To.
Charalene
Lindsy.

REV. G. E. G. BENEOCHRIST
(A DISCIPLE OF JESUS)

THE RESURRECTION OF JESUS CHRIST
(Global Evangelism)

DELIVERANCE ARMY.

PRAYERS
FOR CHILDREN
AND
YOUNG PEOPLE

PRAYERS
FOR CHILDREN
AND
YOUNG PEOPLE

AN ANTHOLOGY

Edited by
NANCY MARTIN

THE WESTMINSTER PRESS
Philadelphia

Published in Great Britain by Hodder and Stoughton
Limited under the title *An Anthology of Prayers for
Children and Young People*

Published by The Westminster Press_®
Philadelphia, Pennsylvania

PRINTED IN THE UNITED STATES OF AMERICA

Library of Congress Cataloging in Publication Data

Main entry under title:

Prayers for children and young people.

    Includes indexes.
    SUMMARY: A collection of prayers for many different occasions.
    1. Children—Prayer-books and devotions—English.
2. Youth—Prayer-books and devotions. 3. Prayers.
[1. Prayers] I. Martin, Nancy.
BV4870.P66 1976   248'.82   75-42383
ISBN 0-664-20746-4

CONTENTS

PREFACE

Any collection of prayers must be, to some extent, a matter of personal preference, but in selecting those of the past as well as the present, I have endeavoured to include a wide range to suit differing needs.

Prayers from the Bible are intentionally limited in number to encourage users of the book to turn to the Bible for further selection. Some hymns which are also prayers have been included, but many more can be found by reference to the numerous hymn books which exist.

I have selected prayers not only for their literary merit but also for their sincerity and aptness of expression for today. The different sections have been arranged to suit the requirements of those responsible for worship in schools, churches, Sunday schools and junior church. The section entitled *Prayers through the Centuries* should be of particular interest for its historical value. It may seem strange to find prayers throughout the book with the more dignified *thy* immediately followed by those which address God more familiarly as *you*, but the compiler may not alter any prayers without the consent of the author or holder of the copyright. However, those who use the prayers can adapt them to suit their particular requirements and taste. This applies particularly to those referred to as *private* or *personal* prayers. If children are encouraged to make their own adaptations of these they will early learn to pray with intelligence and integrity.

I hope that many children and young people will find in this book prayers which they can use in their private devotions and that parents also will find it helpful for bedtime use with their youngest children.

7

If this Anthology assists in drawing children and young people into a closer relationship with the God who knows, loves and cares for them, it will have achieved its purpose.

NANCY MARTIN

Fittleworth
1975

Lord, teach us to pray. *Luke 11/1*

THE LORD'S PRAYER

Our Father which art in heaven,
Hallowed be thy Name,
Thy kingdom come,
Thy will be done, in earth as it is in heaven.
Give us this day our daily bread;
And forgive us our trespasses,
As we forgive them that trespass against us;
And lead us not into temptation,
But deliver us from evil.
For thine is the kingdom, the power, and the glory,
For ever and ever,
Amen.

From The Book of Common Prayer

Our Father in heaven
May your name be honoured
Your kingdom come
Your will be done on earth as in heaven.
Give us each day our daily bread.
Forgive us the wrong we have done
As we forgive others the wrong they have done to us.
Let us not fall when tempted
And save us from evil,
For yours is the kingdom and the power and the glory
for ever.
Amen.

A revised version

Lord, help me!
Matthew 15/25

Speak, Lord, for thy servant heareth!
1 Samuel 3/9

God bless us, every one!
Tiny Tim's Prayer from Dickens Christmas Carol

PRAYERS FOR YOUNGER CHILDREN

Lord teach a little child to pray,
    And then accept my prayer,
Thou hearest all the words I say
    For thou art everywhere.

A little sparrow cannot fall
    Unnoticed, Lord, by thee,
And though I am so young and small
    Thou dost take care of me.

Teach me to do the thing that's right,
    And when I sin, forgive,
And make it still my chief delight
    To serve thee while I live.
            Jane Taylor 1783–1824

Hands together now we lay,
While our little prayer we say,
God be with us all the day—
That is what we pray.
Make us generous in our play,
Kind in all we do or say,
Helping others all the day—
This is what we pray
            A. W. L. Chitty

O Lord God,
Thank you for coming to share our life,
And all its smiles and tears.
You showed us how to live each day
With love that knows no fears.
From God Is Looking After Me
published in aid of handicapped children

Lord Jesus, loving and helpful at home and at school
Help me to be like you.
Lord Jesus, growing up vigorous and strong,
Help me to be like you.
Lord Jesus, working with a will in the carpenter's shop,
Help me to be like you.
Lord Jesus, loving the flowers and the birds, the hills, and the
open sky
Help me to be like you.
Lord Jesus, a friend to everyone,
Help me to be like you.
Lord Jesus, caring for the needs of others,
Help me to be like you.

In Excelsis

Lord of the loving heart,
May mine be loving too,
Lord of the gentle hands,
May mine be gentle too.
Lord of the willing feet,
May mine be willing too,
So may I grow more like to thee
In all I say and do.
All our Days

Dear Father God, you made us all
And every creature, great and small,
Is fed by you and in your care,
Because your love is everywhere.
Mary Osborn

God, this is your world,
    You made us
    You love us;
Teach us how to live
In the world that you have made.
Hope Freeman

Dear Father, who hast all things made,
    And carest for them all,
There's none too great for thy great love,
    Nor anything too small;
If thou canst spend such tender care
    On things that grow so wild,
How wonderful thy love must be
    For me, thy little child.
G. W. Briggs 1875–1959

Lord, when we have not any light,
And mothers are asleep,
Then through the stillness of the night
Thy little children keep.

When shadows haunt the quiet room,
Help us to understand
That thou art with us through the gloom,
To hold us by the hand.
Anne Matheson 1853–1924

Father, we thank thee for the night,
And for the pleasant morning light.
For rest and food and loving care,
And all that makes the day so fair.

Help us to do the things we should,
To be to others kind and good,
In all we do at work or play
To grow more loving every day.
                    Rebecca J. Weston

For the light of my work and play
        Thank you, Heavenly Father.
For the dark of my sleep
For my friends who care for me,
For the animals who play with me
For all your love by night and day
        Thank you, Heavenly Father.

Dear Father God,
Thank you for the Bible.
Thank you for the stories
        about boys and girls
        and grown up people.
Thank you for the songs of praise
        and happy words.
For all the good things in the Bible,
Thank you, Father God.
        Christopher and Margaret Bacon

Thank you for the sunshine bright,
Thank you for the morning light.
        Thank you for the rain and showers
        Thank you for the fruit and flowers.

Thank you for each tall green tree
Thank you for the sand and sea.
    Thank you for the winds that blow
    Thank you for the frost and snow.

Thank you for the beasts so tall
Thank you for the creatures small.
    Thank you for all things that live
    Thank you, God, for all you give.
                    H. Widdows

Dear God,
Thank you for the wind.
For the wind that blows in the trees
And bends their branches to the ground.
The wind that blows the big sailing boats at sea,
And the little ones on the pond.
For the wind that blows the blossom, like snow, in the Spring
And blows the leaves to the ground in the Autumn.
Thank you for the wind that blows in my hair
And all around me.
                    Virginia Salmon

Dear God,
Thank you for the rain.
For the rain that runs and trickles down the window
And makes patterns on the glass.
For the rain that makes the crops and flowers grow
And gives us water to drink.
For rain that blows in our faces and makes our noses wet.
Thank you for the rain that makes big puddles
In which we can jump.
Dear God, thank you for the rain,
And please take care of people who don't have enough rain
    and water to drink, and must go many miles to get it.
                    Virginia Salmon

Dear God
Thank you for the snow.
For the snow that falls so softly and quietly;
For the excited feeling we get when we see it on the ground.
For the crunch of our boots as we walk through it
And the lovely snowmen we can make.
Thank you for the patterns the snow makes on the leaves and
trees
On roof tops and window ledges.
Dear God, thank you for the snow
And please take care of all the old people who don't like it.
Please send someone to help when they are lonely, or too
tired to get in the coal.

Virginia Salmon

Our Father, maker of this wonderful world, thank you for
Saturday, for holiday time and freedom and the open air.
Come into all we are going to do today at home, out of
doors, with our friends.
Help us to enjoy everything you have made for us.

R. S. Macnicol

For cars and planes and trains,
For hikes and holidays,
Thank you, God our Father.
For hobbies, pets and games
For books and 'comics',
Thank you, God our Father.
For TV and the films
For bright shop windows,
Thank you, God our Father.
For play-time and our friends
For fun and laughter,
Thank you, God our Father.
In Excelsis

Thank you, Father God,
 for our holidays.
Thank you for paddling,
 and digging in the sand,
 and going on a boat,
 and sleeping in a caravan,
 and sliding down a slide,
 and playing ball.
Thank you for our Mummies and Daddies,
 and all the people
who gave us a happy holiday.
     Christopher and Margaret Bacon

Thank you, Father God,
 for when we run about out of doors;
 for the green grass in the park,
 and the flowers,
 and the dogs,
 and the people,
 and all the things we love to see.
Thank you, Father God.
     Christopher and Margaret Bacon

Thank you, Father God,
 for when we play in the park (playground)
 for swings
 and slides
 and roundabouts
 and climbing frames.
     Christopher and Margaret Bacon

Thank you, Father God,
 for all the things we see in the street;

cars—buses—shops—stalls—lorries—vans—
traffic lights—crossings—so many things.
We love to go for walks in the street.
Thank you for all we see.

Christopher and Margaret Bacon

For our warm homes,
the food we eat,
the clothes we wear,
our cosy beds,
Thank you, God.

Christopher and Margaret Bacon

Dear Father God,
Thank you for our new clothes.
Thank you for the people who make them,
and the shop people who sell them,
and our Mummies and Daddies who buy them for us
Thank you for nice new clothes to wear.

Christopher and Margaret Bacon

Thank you, Father God,
for our Mummies and Daddies,
and our Grannies and Grandads.
They look after us,
and play with us.
They make our breakfast
and our dinner
and our tea.
They take us out for walks,
and tuck us up at bedtime.
For all the nice things they do,
Thank you, God.

Christopher and Margaret Bacon

God bless all the Aunties
    Who are kind to girls and boys;
God bless all the Uncles
    Who remember birthday toys.

And if there is a little child
    In this wide world alone
Who has not any family
    To call his very own,

Then may God send a blessing
    Of a very special kind,
To bring a happy day
    And leave a memory behind.
Kathleen Patridge

God bless all those that I love;
God bless all those that love me:
God bless all those that love those that I love
And all those that love those that love me.
From an old New England sampler

Dear Lord God our Father, maker of all things,
    make our lives bright and beautiful today,
    bright with truthful speaking,
    beautiful with loving and happy deeds.
Teach us how we can change sad places into glad ones.
Teach us how to let you come into this world,
    so that everyone may love to do all things well.
R. S. Macnicol

O God our loving Father,
Bless us at school today,
And help us to be attentive;

Bless us at home today,
And help us to be obedient;
Bless us at games today,
And help us to be unselfish;
Bless us at meals today,
And help us to be thankful;
For Jesus' sake.
John Oxenham and Roderic Dunkerley

Holy God who madest me
And all things else to worship thee;
Keep me fit in mind and heart,
Body and soul to take my part.
Fit to stand, and fit to run,
Fit for sorrow, fit for fun,
Fit for work and fit for play,
Fit to face life day by day,
Holy God who madest me,
Make me fit to worship thee.

Teach us, our Father, to give ourselves to you
    as Jesus did, without being mean or selfish.
Help us to think always of what others need;
Help us to share what we have with others.
You have given us so many good things;
We thank you most of all for the love of Jesus,
    the greatest gift of all.
                              R. S. Macnicol

O Lord, may each one who has to do with us today
    be the happier for it.
Give us the wisdom of a loving heart that we may
    say the right thing in the right way.

Give us a quick eye for little kindnesses,
    that we may be ready in doing them,
    and gracious in receiving them.
Help us to understand the feelings and
    needs of other people, and
    make us eager-hearted in helping them;
    for Christ's sake.

Brownie-Guide Prayer Book

First the seed,
And then the grain;
Thank you, God,
For sun and rain.

First the flour,
And then the bread;
Thank you, God,
That we are fed.

First your love,
And then your giving;
Show us, God,
Your way of living.

Thank you, God,
For all your care;
Help us all,
To share and share.

Lilian Cox

Dear Lord Jesus,
Thank you for the work we have done today,
For the exercise it has given our minds;
For the pleasure we have had from it.

Help us always to enjoy our work, whatever it is,
    and to do it with all our hearts
    to your praise and glory.

Please bless those who have no work
    especially if they have had none for a long time.
They must be very bored and unhappy.
Please help their families to help them
    and give them some work to do soon.

Graham Salmon

Almighty Father, giver of life and health, guide and help all those who are trying to make our roads safer.

Help those who drive and ride and walk on our roads to be patient, unselfish and thoughtful of others, so that everyone may travel in safety.

Hope Freeman

Heavenly Father, it's very wet and windy tonight and it will be blowing a gale out at sea. We pray that you will bless and guard the sailors who bring us our food and so many things we need; and the fishermen who bring us the harvest of the sea. Help them to be alert to the dangers of rough seas and bring them safe home to their families.

Graham Salmon

Dear Lord Jesus, the fire engine went by today sounding its hooter, on its way to a fire. We thank you for the firemen who put the welfare of others before their own; who bravely risk their own lives to rescue others. We pray for those who have lost homes or relatives in a fire. And we pray for ourselves—that we may not, by any carelessness, put others at risk.

Graham Salmon

Please God, take care of little things,
The fledglings that have not their wings,
Till they are big enough to fly
And stretch their wings across the sky.

And please take care of little seeds
So small among the forest weeds
Till they have grown as tall as trees
With leafy boughs, take care of these.

And please take care of drops of rain
Like beads upon a broken chain,
Till in some river in the sun
The many silver drops are one.

Take care of small new lambs that bleat,
Small foals that totter on their feet,
And all small creatures ever known
Till they are strong to stand alone.

And please take care of children who
Kneel down at night to pray to you,
Oh please keep safe the little prayer
That like the big ones asks your care.

Eleanor Farjeon

THE PRAYER OF THE LITTLE BIRD
Dear God,
I don't know how to pray by myself very well,

but will you please
protect my little nest from wind and rain?
Put a great deal of dew on the flowers,
many seeds in my way.
Make your blue very high,
Your branches lissom;
let your kind light stay late in the sky
and set my heart brimming with such music
that I must sing, sing, sing . . .
Please Lord.

Carmen Bernos de Gasstold
Translated from the French by
Rumer Godden

Private Prayers

Dear Father God, I want to pray to you, but I don't know how. Please God, be my friend and help me to like everybody and not be selfish and bad-tempered, and I will love you and try to do the things you want me to do.

N.M.

Dear Lord Jesus, are you listening, because I'm going to say my prayers just as if I were talking to Mummy and Daddy. I've done some naughty things today. It's hard to say I'm sorry but I truly am. Please God, forgive me and help me to be better tomorrow.

N.M.

Guard me by day
Guard me by night
Guard me when mother
Blows out the light.

Now I wake and see the light
'Tis God has kept me through the night
To him I lift my voice and pray
That he will keep me through the day.

Be with me, Lord, all through this day,
And make me good, and keep me true;
Help me in all I think and say,
And teach me what I ought to do.

Elfreyda M. C. Wightman

Dear Lord Jesus, thank you for a lovely new day with lots of exciting things to do for you. Please help me to choose the ones you would like me to do and not to do anything that would hurt or grieve you. When bedtime comes, let me look back on a happy day without anything in it to make me sorry or ashamed. Because I have asked you to help me I know you will. Thank you, Jesus.

Nina Hinchy

Dear God, this new day is like a clean page in a book. Help me to fill it with the beauty of kind words, helpful actions and unselfish thoughts, and may I not spoil it with ugly and unkind deeds.

Phyllis Lovelock

Now evening has come, dear God. So many things have happened and the page of my book is full. I hope your eyes of love will find some beauty on it, and please forgive the blots and smudges.

Phyllis Lovelock

Dear Lord Jesus, thank you for taking care of me and loving me all through this day. I know that I have not been as good as I should all the time. Sometimes I have been lazy or disobedient and wanted my own way. Sometimes I have been quarrelsome and lost my temper. I have been greedy and selfish, wanting all the best things for myself. Please forgive me and help me to be better tomorrow. Thank you, Lord Jesus, for everything good and lovely today, but most of all, thank you for yourself and your great love for me.

Nina Hinchy

My Father hear my prayer
Before I go to rest;
It is thy little child
That cometh to be blest.

Lord, help me every day
To love thee more and more
And try to do thy will
Much better than before.

Now look upon me, Lord,
Ere I lie down to rest;
It is thy little child
That cometh to be blest.
Virginia Kimber

Father God, I want to say thank you for all the things you have given me today. Thank you for games and toys and for friends to play with. Thank you for the food I've had and all the other good things you have given, and help me to think of others who are not as fortunate as I am.

Thank you most of all for Mummy and Daddy and all my relations and thank you for listening to me.

N.M.

Dear Father, whom I cannot see,
I know that you are near to me.
Quite quietly I speak to you:
Please show me what you'd have me do.
Please help me plan kind things to do
For other people and for you.
Thank you for always helping me,
Dear Father, whom I cannot see.

Lilian Cox

For home and those who love me,
    For all my books and toys,
For all the fun I have at play
    With other girls and boys:

For flowers in the garden,
    For laden apple trees,
For dogs and cats and ponies,
    I thank thee, Lord, for these.

And if I do not thank thee
    As often as I should,
Help me to thank thee truly
    By trying to be good.

Elfrida Vipont

Dear God our Father,
Thank you for my Mummy and Daddy. Please bless and help all the children who have no Mummies or Daddies and give them an extra special bit of your love.

N.M.

Dear Lord Jesus, there's a new baby in our home. Thank you for sending him. Mummy and Daddy and I are very happy and I am to be his big brother/sister.

I have always wanted a little brother/sister. Thank you, Jesus, for sending us this one. Please help me to take great care of him/her, to play happily, to share my toys and not be jealous.

Nina Hinchy

Please God, bless all new babies and help them to grow big and strong. Help their Mummies and Daddies to care for them and teach them about you and your love for them.

N.M.

Dear Lord Jesus, thank you for loving me so much and wanting me to love you too. You are everybody's best friend, so you are my best friend. Please help me to be just the sort of friend you would like to have. Though I am very naughty sometimes I really do love you and want to make you happy.

Nina Hinchy

Dear God, please bless my Mummy and Daddy who have given me such a happy birthday. I have enjoyed everything so much. Thank you for giving me a Mummy to make me a birthday cake and a Daddy who can mend toys if they break or go wrong. There are lots of boys and girls who do not have a special fuss made when it is their birthday. Show me if there is anyone like that in my road or school so that I can be specially nice to them.

Beryl Bye

Dear God, they say I've been a naughty boy this week, but I think you'll understand. You see, my Daddy died, and it's left an awful gap. We loved him such a lot. It made my Mummy cry, and my little sister, too. Boys are not supposed to cry, but I did blub a bit.

Why did you let him die, dear God? It made me very cross with you. 'I'll never speak to God again,' I said. But Mum explained that you had other, more important work for Dad to do. She said you'd want me to be brave and try to take Dad's place.

I'm trying awfully hard, but it isn't easy, God, you know. So please forgive me for my naughty words, and help me to understand.

N.M.

Dear Lord Jesus, our little dog has died. We cried because she was so loving and good. She made everyone happy. We are glad it's you who've got her now. Please take care of her, but of course you will. You love all animals. You made them all.

Thank you for letting us have her first and for all the happy times we've had with her.

Nina Hinchy

Forgive me for the angry words
    I didn't mean to say,
Forgive me for the fit of sulks,
    That spoiled a happy day.

Forgive me for the muddle
    That I left upon the floor,
The tea I wouldn't eat,
    The hasty way I slammed the door.

THANKSGIVING AND PRAISE

For eyes whereby I clearly see
The many lovely things there be;
For lungs to breathe the morning air,
For nose to smell its fragrance rare;
For tongue to taste the fruits that grow,
For birds that sing and flowers that blow;
For limbs to climb, and swim, and run,
For skin to feel the cheerful sun;
For sun and moon and stars in heaven,
Whose gracious light is freely given;
The river where the green weed floats,
And where I sail my little boats;
The sea, where I can bathe and play,
The sands where I can race all day;
The pigeons wheeling in the sun,
Who fly more quickly than I run;
The winds that sing as they rush by,
The clouds that race across the sky;
The shelter of the shady woods,
Where I may spend my lonely moods;
The gabled house that is my home,
The garden where I love to roam,
And bless my parents, every day,
Though they be very far away,
Take thou my thanks, O God above,
For all these tokens of thy love.
And when I am a man do thou
Make me as grateful then as now.
                    Richard Molesworth Dennis
                    who died in the 1914–18 war

O God, we thank thee for this earth, our home; for the wide sky and the blessed sun, for the salt sea and the running water, for the everlasting hills and the never-resting winds, for trees and the common grass underfoot. We thank thee for our senses by which we hear the songs of birds, and see the splendour of the summer fields, and taste of the autumn fruits, and rejoice in the feel of the snow, and smell the breath of the spring. Grant us a heart wide open to all this beauty and save our souls from being so blind that we pass unseeing when even the common thornbush is aflame with thy glory; O God, our Creator, who livest and reignest for ever and ever.

Walter Rauschenbusch

O God, who hast made this great world, the sun and the moon and the stars; we thank thee for this wonderful earth, filled with all that we need for life. Teach us how to discover what is good and useful for everyone. Bless what men invent and use so that there is enough for everyone's need.

R. S. Macnicol

We thank thee, O Father, for the sun that warms us and the air that gives us life; for all the beauty of earth, in field and hedgerow, brook and covert, woods and hills; for the changing seasons, each in its order beautiful; for our homes; for health of body and mind; for the land we love; for freedom and just laws; for the lives and examples of the good and brave of every age and every race; and for the life on earth of Jesus, our example, who came to show us how to live.

Hymns and Prayers for Dragons

Thank you, God for giving me so much—
    my home and family and friends
    my strong and healthy body

the interesting and beautiful world in which I live
books to read—music to listen to
a school where I can learn
Christians with whom to worship
a church where we can meet.

Above all—I thank you for loving me,
For sending your Son into the world to show me how to live.

Forgive me
    when I ask you for too much—
    when I forget to thank you for what I already have.
Forgive me, too, when I am selfish and demanding—
    when I want to GET more than I want to GIVE.
                Brother Kenneth and Sister Geraldine

For these and all your gifts, Lord,
    We thank you.
For health, and strength, and life itself,
    We thank you.
For our friends, our homes, our families,
    We thank you.
For our church and our worship,
    We thank you.
For every chance to serve you,
    We thank you.
For Jesus Christ our Lord,
    We thank you.
And now we pray for all who govern our land,
    We ask you to bless them.
For all who minister in our church,
    We ask you to bless them.
For all who provide our daily needs,
    We ask you to bless them.

For all who do not yet know you,
> *We ask you to bless them.*

For all who are tired, or ill, or lonely,
> *We ask you to bless them.*

Hear these prayers, Lord our God, for Jesus' sake.
> *Christopher Idle*

For all the men and women, boys and girls, who love and serve you,
> *We thank you God.*

For everybody who makes Jesus real to other people,
> *We thank you God.*

For everyone who has taught about you by the way they think, the way they act and by what they say,
> *We thank you God.*

For everyone who helps those who are sick or sad, and for all those who are brave and patient when things are going wrong,
> *We thank you God.*

Dear God, may we know you better and better so that we may love you more and more and serve you with all our hearts.
> *Please God hear us.*

May we help those in need; may they know that God is real and that God is love,
> *Please God hear us.*

May we be friends with you, friends with all your children, friends with one another.
> *Please God hear us.*

> *Dick Williams*

We praise thee, O Father,
> For the beauty of this world, our home; for the glory of sunrise and sunset, the song of the birds, the wind in the trees, and the gaiety of flowers.

34

We praise thy name, O Lord,

For the goodness of life; for the stir of youth in our veins, for our health and the power to achieve.
For those who are without health and without hope we pray.

For our friends without whose company life would be the poorer.
For those who are lonely and without joy we pray.

For thy presence in the common things of life, in games, good comradeship, pure laughter and loving kindness.
For those whose life is hard and who have never learnt to know thee we pray.

For thy love to us, for thy eternal friendship; making this world our home, this earth our heaven.
That we may help others to know thy friendship and find their true home we pray.

For the great tasks to which we are called, which will test all our courage and loyalty and love, and because in loyalty to that which is difficult lies our true manhood, we praise thee.

Youth at Worship

Let us praise God in gladness and humility for all great and simple joys. For games and holidays in the open air, for the joy of work attempted and achieved; for books and pictures and all our small possessions; for all pure comedy and laughter; for the gift of humour and gaiety of heart. For the image of Christ in ordinary people; their forbearance and good temper, their courage and their kindness. For all holy and humble men of heart through whom the loveliness of our Saviour Christ has been made manifest to the world.

The Kingdom, the Power and the Glory

For food and friends my thanks I give;
Now grant me grace to strive
To thank thee every hour I live,
Because I am alive.

Geddes Macgregor

Heavenly Father, we thank you for our homes and families, for our food and clothing, and for all the happiness that parents and children can share. We ask that your love may surround us, your care protect us and that we may know your peace at all times, for Jesus' sake.

M. H. Botting

We thank you, God for our homes:
Our mothers and fathers, our brothers and sisters
And the others in our family;
For all our friends in the same road (or across the back street, or, as appropriate 'in the same block').
Help us to love and be friends with all of them;
To have no fighting, no quarrels, no bitter thoughts;
But to behave in such a way that everyone else may be glad to have us living near them;
In the name of Jesus Christ, whom boys and girls were always glad to meet.

Christopher Idle

Let us give thanks
For friends and home,
For work and play,
For hands to make, and eyes to see, and lips to speak,
For strength to do our daily task
And, at the end, the gift of quiet sleep.

A. M. Ammon

THANKSGIVING AND PRAISE

Bread is a lovely thing to eat—
God bless the barley and the wheat;
A lovely thing to breathe is air—
God bless the sunshine everywhere;
The earth's a lovely place to know—
God bless the folks that come and go!
Alive's a lovely thing to be—
Giver of life—we say—bless thee!

Child Education

Dear Father God, thank you for the lovely countryside around us. May we do nothing to spoil your wonderful handiwork. Help us to make our village a beautiful place. Show us how to fill it with kind deeds and loving words. Let it be the kind of village that brings you honour and glory.

Brenda Holloway

Then let us praise the Father, who shows us, of his grace,
The secret paths of science, the mastery of space,
The wonder of the wireless, of TV, cars and trains,
For man made these, but God made man,
And God gave man his brains.

Mrs. Lesbia Scott

THE SEASONS

Praise the Lord for all the beauty
Coming with the blossoming spring.
Praise the Lord for summer showers;
Praise him for the birds that sing.
Praise the Lord for golden harvest,
Winter frost and white snowfall.
Praise him, praise him when December
Brings his Christmas festival.
Elizabeth Gould

O God, we want to praise and thank you for giving us so much to enjoy in your world. Open our eyes to see all the beauty around us, to appreciate your greatness in giving us the different seasons, each fulfilling our needs. And if we do not understand why nature is sometimes cruel and harsh, and why people suffer from earthquakes and other disasters in your world, help us to trust where we cannot see, knowing that you love us all. Help us to do what we can to relieve the sufferings and hardships caused by these disasters and those caused by human errors.

Make us willing and eager to share the many good things you have provided for the benefit of all.

N.M.

We praise thy name, O Father, for the beauty of the springtime and the summer, the glory of the sky by day and night, the healthful wind and quickening rain. We thank thee for the bloom and fragrance of the flowers, the songs of birds, the joyousness of every living thing.

In all that thou has made we see the wonder of thy wisdom and thy care, who clothest the grass of the field and takest thought for the sparrows. Help us to trust thy never-failing goodness, the love which is beyond our understanding, and surrounds our lives with blessing.

God, who touchest earth with beauty,
Make me lovely too;
With thy Spirit re-create me,
Make my heart anew.

Like thy springs and running waters,
Make me crystal pure;
Like thy rocks of towering grandeur,
Make me strong and sure.

Like thy dancing waves in sunlight,
Make me glad and free;
Like the straightness of the pine-trees,
Let me upright be.

Like the arching of the heavens,
Lift my thoughts above;
Turn my dreams to noble action—
Ministries of love.

God, who touchest earth with beauty,
Make me lovely too;
Keep me ever, by thy Spirit,
Pure and strong and true.

Mary S. Edgar

We give thee thanks, Lord of heaven and earth, for the
promise of summer, for the beauty of this day—a day
    that shall ripen grain,
    that shall provide good things for the table,
    that shall make all growing things rejoice,
    that shall make more sweet the music of the birds,
    that shall make more beautiful the gardens which thou
      hast planted and watered.
We thank thee for the fertility of the land that encourages
us to sow and to plant. We thank thee for the dependence
of the seasons, for all thy sustaining providence by which
men work today and harvest tomorrow.
We well know, our Father, that we are not worthy of thy
bounty, but help us to be good stewards of that bounty.
We thank thee for the endless delight of our lives on this
lovely earth.

Peter Marshall

For all the rich autumnal glories spread—
The flaming pageant of the ripening woods,
The fiery gorse, the heather-purpled hills;
The rustling leaves that fly before the wind
And lie below the hedgerows whispering;
For meadows silver-white with hoary dew;
The first crisp breath of wonder in the air
We thank thee, Lord.

Dear God, who made the world, we thank you for the
winter. We thank you for the cold frosty days, when we
jump and run and keep warm; for snow, and the fun we have
with it; for warm clothes and good fires and hot dinners. And
especially we thank you for the wonderful time of Christmas
when you sent us your own Son as a baby to show us how
much you love us all.

SPECIAL DAYS

Christmas
O God, our Loving Father, we are so happy that Christmas is coming again. Help us to remember that it is the birthday of Jesus. We thank you for sending Jesus to teach us about you, and to show us how to lead brave and adventurous lives. Please help us to grow more like him, and help us to praise him in our carols, and in our happiness and laughter and fun.

Brenda Holloway

O Lord Jesus Christ, come and dwell in my heart this Christmas-tide, so that our home may have you in it and be full of joy and peace. May no ill-temper, impatience, envy or jealousy spoil the gladness of your birthday, but may love shine in our midst, bringing warmth and light to all our hearts and minds.

J. M. Macdougall Ferguson

Let us thank God for Christmas:
For this happy and exciting time of the year
Thank you loving Father.
For Christmas trees and decorations
Thank you loving Father.
For cards and presents and good food
Thank you loving Father.
For fun with family and friends
Thank you loving Father.

For singing carols and listening to the Christmas story
Thank you loving Father.
For all these things because we have them to remind us of the
coming of Jesus
Thank you loving Father.

J. D. Searle

We thank you, Heavenly Father, for sending your only Son, Jesus Christ, to become part of the family of man. We thank you for Mary and Joseph who looked after him and guarded and protected him when he was little. We thank you for bringing him to manhood so that in all his earthly life we can see what you are like. We thank you for reminding us at Christmas how much you love us, and for helping us to realise that you always have loved us and always will. Help us to love and serve you gladly in return, through Jesus Christ our Lord.

Dick Williams

Heavenly Father, please comfort the people who won't be happy this Christmas: those who won't get any presents, or even any Christmas cards; those who won't have the money to buy the presents they would love to give their friends; those who won't have a Christmas dinner, or won't get the things they are longing for; and those who will be sad because someone they love will not be with them.

Zinnia Bryan

Dear Father thank you for Jesus; for his birth and all that this has meant to people all over the world for nearly two thousand years. Help us to grow like him day by day. Help us to make other people happy, as he did, and to do what you would wish us to do.

As we enjoy ourselves this Christmas we remember all the

healing love which Jesus brought into the world for us and for people everywhere.

N.M.

> Lord, to those who never listened
> To the message of thy birth
> Who have winter, but no Christmas
> Bringing them thy peace on earth,
> Send to these the joyful tidings;
> By all people, in each home,
> Be there heard the Christmas anthem,
> Praise to God, the Christ has come.
>
> *George Stringer Rowe*

Sorry, full up! No room here!
Not a hope! Go away!

Lord, we remember that when you first came to earth there was no room for you.

No one spared a thought for the condition of your mother;
No one thought of anyone but themselves.
The world hasn't changed much, Lord;
Human nature hasn't changed much either.
Lord, forgive our unwillingness to find a place for you in our crowded lives.
Forgive our love of self which sees our wellbeing as all important.
Forgive our corporate neglect of the homeless, the destitute, the under-privileged, the unfortunate, who like you have nowhere to lay their heads.

Lord, forgive what we have been, amend what we are, direct what we shall become, for the sake of Jesus Christ our Lord.

Gordon Bates

43

New Year

Another year has gone, O Father, and as we look back we see how full of faults it has been. We are truly sorry and wish that we had tried harder to do well. We thank thee that we have another chance to try again, and we pray thee that thou wilt give us the strength to do better. Help us, no matter what comes in this new year, to do our best. If illness comes, let us bear it bravely; if disappointment comes, let us learn to go to thee for comfort; if joy comes let it make us all the more ready to try and give joy to other people. Bless us now, O Lord, and all through the year, through Jesus Christ our Lord.

Selina Fitzherbert Fox

O God, our Father, be with us as we start a New Year. We do not know what the new year holds in store for us, but we do know that you will love us and will help us whenever we ask you. Guide us through the coming months. Help us to grow more like Jesus, so that we may go about helping people as he did. When we are happy, may we remember to thank you. Help us to bear our disappointments bravely, and show us how to be cheerful and full of courage. May your spirit fill our homes, O Father, making them happy and full of good temper because we are trying to do your will.

Brenda Holloway

Palm Sunday

Father, on this Palm Sunday, we too would offer our praise to thy great name. Accept, we pray, the things we are able to offer, however small and insignificant, and give thy blessing to them. As we listen to the stories of thy love may we be stirred to follow in thy pathway of love. Help us throughout the week and always to serve thee in gladness and truth.

Doris W. Street

Good Friday

O Lord Jesus, as we face the cross today, we wonder at your love for us. We can never deserve what you did for us on this day. Looking at the people who brought about your death we can see so many of the same faults in ourselves, and we are sorry for them. By faith we gladly take the forgiveness you offer us from your cross, and through the door you pushed open then, we come back into God's family where we really belong.

Leslie R. Earnshaw

O God, we think today of your great goodness and love as shown in the suffering of Jesus. You allowed him to die on the cross that we might know how to live; might know that same love and forgiveness is ours. Help us to accept this and make us more worthy of it.

N.M.

Easter

     For the deep wonder of the Good Friday story;
     For love that did not falter,
     For love that was ready to die,
     For love that carries the burden of our sin,
     For love too great for us to glimpse or guess;
        We praise thee, Lord of life.

     For the glory of Easter Sunday;
     For shame transformed to splendour,
     For fellowship unbroken,
     For gladness out of sorrow;
     For life out of death;
        We praise thee, Lord of life.

Lilian Cox

Resurrection

Because you come back to your friends, who thought you
were dead
We praise you, Easter Lord.

Because you are alive for always, as truly with us every day
as ever you were with them:
We praise you, Easter Lord.

Because you came in love and holiness and nearness; because
you spoke a woman's name, and lit a picnic fire to cook
breakfast:
We praise you, Easter Lord.

Because you have shown us that God's love is stronger far
than death; and because you have promised to share with
us your life beyond the grave:
We praise you, Easter Lord.

Because your love is stronger than anything else in the
universe; and because, through that love, you died and
rose again for us:
We praise you, Easter Lord.

Lilian Cox

Can it be true, the things they say of you?
You walked this earth sharing with friends you knew
All that they had, the work, the joy, the pain,
That we might find the way to heav'n again.

And day by day you still return this way;
But we recall there was a debt to pay;
Out of your love for your own world above
You left that holy thing, your endless love to prove.

Can it be true, the things they did to you—
The death, the shame, and were your friends so few?
Yet you returned again alive and free—
Can it be true, my Lord, it had to be.

Brother William SSF

Ascension Day

Lord Jesus, we remember how you returned to your Father on the first Ascension Day. Although we cannot see you with our eyes, we know that you are still with us as you promised always to be. We thank you for being our constant friend. Help us to remember that we can always come to you and that you will never fail us. Help us to come to you when we are frightened or disappointed, and may we remember to tell you about our joys as well as our troubles.

Brenda Holloway

I wonder how you would do it nowadays?
Then, you took your eleven friends for a walk
And when you disappeared in the cloud
They knew you were saying goodbye to them.
They had to get used to the idea that they
    weren't going to see you any more,
    as they had done for nearly three years.
But they had your promise
'Remember I am with you always,
To the end of time.'

It's wonderful to know you are around,
I don't have to go to a special place,
Or say particular words—
Or even feel in the right mood.
'I am with you always,' you said.
I hope I remember that—at least sometimes.

Brother Kenneth and Sister Geraldine

Whitsun

Lord, on the first Whit Sunday your disciples received the Holy Spirit and went out boldly to tell people of your love. Help us boldly to choose to do that which is right and so show
we are your followers too.

Phyllis Lovelock

Birthdays

It is my birthday, Lord Jesus, my Saviour, and I thank thee for giving me the wonderful gift of life. I pray that I may use my life rightly, that I may try to grow braver, kinder, wiser and truer year by year. I thank thee for all the joys of the past year, and pray thee to bless me through the coming one. Help me to conquer my faults and live more to thy praise. Grant me thy grace to help all those around me, and to try and make them happy. Be with me step by step all through this new year, and keep me safe unto the end.

Selina Fitzherbert Fox

O God, I want to thank you for giving me this birthday and for all the love and happiness that it will hold. Please help me to begin a new year today, and to love you and everyone who loves me much more than I did before. Help me to be unselfish and to share all my pleasures as Jesus would like me to do, for his holy and loving sake.

Prayers for Little Children

Holidays

O God we're excited that at last this day has come —
we've been thinking about it for a long time,
we've been saving up for it;
we've been waiting for this moment.

We are glad that you have made the world so full of nice
places;
    so full of trees and mountains and rivers and seas;
    so full of little creatures and great; little children and
       men and women to know;
    so full of healthy, exciting things to do that we haven't
       done yet;
Keep us safe in our journeying, unselfish in our interests,
kind in our thoughts;
And don't let us spoil any of the good things and places we
enjoy with damage, or litter, or fire;
And bring us home again when it's time, refreshed and sun-
browned and strong.

Rita Snowden

World Children's Day

Dear Father God, today we think of other boys and girls
throughout the world. Some are not so fortunate as we
are. Bless all children who live in difficult and dangerous
places; who do not always have enough to eat; who live
in crowded houses, and have nowhere to play; who have
no parents or whose parents are not always kind and
thoughtful.

Bless those children who do not see beautiful things
around them; who do not have holidays, or fun with their
families.

Bless them, Lord, and help all those people who are trying
to help them and make their lives happier.

Help us not to forget them, as we grow older, and can take
our place in this world that we share.

Jean Stevens

Harvest

We dare not ask you bless our harvest feast
Till it is spread for poorest and for least,
We dare not bring our harvest gifts to you
Unless our hungry brothers share them too.

Not only at this time, Lord; every day
Those whom you love are dying while we pray.
Teach us to do with less, and so to share,
From our abundance more than we can spare.

Now with this harvest plenty round us piled,
Show us the Christ in every starving child;
Speak, as you spoke of old in Galilee,
'You feed, or you refuse, not them but me!'

Lilian Cox

O Lord of the harvest,
    Send labourers into thy field
Send some to reap,
    And some to sow,
And some to clear the ground
    And plough;
And if thou wilt
    Send me.

Rt. Rev. Bishop E. S. Woods

Give, O Lord, to all who till the ground, the wisdom to
understand thy laws, and to co-operate with the wise ordering
of the world. Give to men of science the power to discover
the secrets of nature. Give to farmers and labourers the desire
to work together in the spirit of justice and goodwill. And
grant that the fruits of thy bountiful earth may not be
hoarded by selfish men, or squandered by foolish men, but

that all who work may share abundantly in the harvest of thy soil, according to thy will, revealed to us in Jesus Christ our Lord.

The Kingdom, the Power and the Glory

A TOWN CHILD'S THANKS FOR HARVEST
Dear Father God,
Thank you for the shops in my street.
I look in the windows, and see so many lovely things.
Thank you for gardeners and farmers who grow things,
    fat green marrows, shining piles of apples,
      brown potatoes with the smell of the earth upon them.
Thank you for people who live in other lands, who grow
   things for me;
Rice and grapes, and sugar, melons, coffee and tea.

Thank you for sailors who work in ships, and men who work
   in the docks, or drive great lorries, or push barrows in the
   markets.

Thank you, God, for everyone who grows my food and
   prepares it for me.
Help boys and girls who are not as fortunate as I, who live in
   lands where there is not much water, where the soil is not
   good, and it is hard for things to grow.

Help me, God, to share the good things that I have.

Jean Stevens

WORSHIP

For a New School Term

Dear God, for those boys and girls who are starting school today we ask a special blessing. Their new life will seem very strange to most of them. Some will be shy and feel lost and lonely among so many other boys and girls. Some will be eager to learn; others will find it difficult. Help us to be friendly and do what we can to make them happy and wanted, for Jesus' sake, who is the children's friend.

N.M.

Lord on this new term
We ask your blessing
For each and everyone of us
As we return to school.
Teach us to learn,
Our faults confessing,
And give your peace of mind
And guidance to us all.
Virginia Salmon

Dear God, entering the sixth form is a big step in our school life. With so many new things to learn and new ways of learning them, there will be much we shall find very difficult. Help us to become neither discouraged, nor self-satisfied, but always to strive to do better, and to work to our full ability, helping and learning from each other. As sixth formers we will have new liberties and new responsibilities.

Teach us to respect our liberties and be willing to accept our responsibilities, always remembering not only that we are setting a standard for our school, but that we were first formers once.

Dear God, these two years have so much to offer us, can be so much fun and so very satisfying. Please help us to use them well, and be with us all.

Virginia Salmon

We pray, dear Father, that thou wilt bless all those who create beauty in the world,
    the artists and musicians,
    the sculptors and designers,
    those who plan our towns,
    those who guard the beauty of the countryside,
    those who give light to all who sit in darkness.
Guard and strengthen them, our Father, and may we, in our own time, be thy servants in the realms of beauty.

A. Murray Smith

School Assembly

O Lord, our heavenly Father, by whose Spirit man is taught knowledge, who givest wisdom to all them that ask thee, we beseech thee to prosper all colleges and schools of sound learning; and especially, to bless all who serve thee here, whether as teachers or learners. Help us to labour diligently and faithfully, remembering that without thee we can do nothing and that in thy fear is the beginning of wisdom. Open our eyes to know thy marvellous works, and enlighten our minds that we may understand the wondrous things of thy law. Enable us to set thy holy will ever before us, that so our fellows, now and in the days to come, may be the better for our studies here. Finally we pray for all those who have gone forth from this school, that they may be so guided and strengthened by thy Spirit that being true disciples of Jesus Christ, they may live blameless and faithful lives to the glory of thy holy name.

John Hunter 1849–1917

Father, we hold before you now in prayer our life together in this school.

Help us to give to it of our best, and to receive in turn the best it has to give.

Teach us to know the joys of discovery, the warmth of friendship, the satisfaction of attempting and achieving, and the demands of truth.

Open for us week by week new windows on our world; increase our understanding of ourselves and others.

May teachers and taught alike seek first your Kingdom, to the good of this school and the glory of your Name.

Timothy Dudley-Smith

We build our school on thee, O Lord,
To thee we bring our common need,
The loving heart, the helpful word,
The tender thought, the kindly deed;
With these we pray
Thy Spirit may
Enrich and bless our school alway.

We work together in thy sight,
We live together in thy love;
Guide thou our faltering steps aright,
And lift our thoughts to heaven above;
Dear Lord, we pray
Thy Spirit may
Be present in our school alway.

Hold thou each hand to keep it just;
Teach thou our lips, and make them pure;
If thou art with us, Lord, we must
Be faithful friends and comrades sure;
Dear Lord, we pray
Thy Spirit may
Be present in our school alway.

We change but thou art still the same,
The same, good Master, Teacher, Friend,
We change, but, Lord, we bear thy name,
To journey with it to the end;
And so we pray
Thy Spirit may
Be present in our school alway.

S. W. Meyer

Go with us, our Father, throughout this day. In our work
strengthen us; in our study enlighten us; and may all that
we say and all that we do be as thou would have it.

A. Murray Smith

Almighty Father, we pray thy blessing upon all whom thou
hast joined together in the brotherhood of this school. Grant
that we may so work and play, think and pray together, that
we may be more perfectly fitted to serve thee and our brothers
in the work to which thou shalt call us. Help us to look wide,
fill us with high ideals, inspire us with love and goodwill to
all men; that we may rightly lead others in the paths of
chivalry and honour, ourselves following in the steps of him
who died in the service of men, thy Son, our Saviour, Jesus
Christ.

Toc H Prayer. Rev. George Moore

O God, we give thee thanks for all who use their lives to help other people.

For the courage and adventurous spirit of explorers and inventors:
We thank thee, O Lord.

For the knowledge and skill of scientists and engineers:
We thank thee, O Lord.

For the faith and unselfishness of doctors, nurses, and teachers:
We thank thee, O Lord.

For the imagination and patience of writers, musicians, and artists:
We thank thee, O Lord.

For the willing service of all who work to supply our daily needs:
We thank thee, O Lord.

For the love of all who take care of us:
We thank thee, O Lord.

For the joy of being able to use our gifts and strength to serve thee:
We thank thee, O Lord.

Brownie-Guide Prayer Book

Almighty God, who lovest all mankind, help us to make the world a better and cleaner place, and a fitter dwelling for thy children upon earth.

O Lord, bless our school;
That, working together
And playing together,
We may learn to serve thee
And to serve one another.
A. M. Ammon

Thank you, our Father God, for our school, where we learn about the world you made, and how to live in it. Thank you for the lessons we learn, the games we play, the stories we hear, and the songs we sing. Thank you for hard work done; for difficult things won, and for all our fun.

John Oxenham and Roderic Dunkerley 1853–1941

End of Term

O God, we bring to thee at the close of this term, our humble and hearty thanks for all the blessings we have received; for health and strength, for the opportunities of improving our talents, for progress we have been enabled to make, for any success we have gained, and for the joys of friendship. Forgive us for those things wherein we have failed; our yielding to temptation, our slackness, our neglect, our unfaithfulness. May the holidays bring us increased strength so that we may return here more ready to pursue our studies with renewed vigour and to render thee more loyal service. Be with those of our number whose schooldays have now come to an end. As they take their place as workers in the world, may they seek to serve, not with eye service as man-pleasers, but as servants of Christ, doing the will of God.

R. J. Shambrook

Almighty God, help us to take with us into our holidays the lessons that we have here learnt, of modesty and self-denial, of truth and honour, of unselfish service for something bigger than ourselves. In the changed circumstances of holiday life may we show that we know the meaning and the value of these things. And from the sun and the hills and the open air, from new friendships and new experiences, may we bring back next term new inspiration, new wisdom, new strength, and a new determination to work together and to live together for the good of the whole and for thee.

M. L. Jacks

On Going into Church

O God, I am in thy house. Teach me to pray to thee, and praise thee. Keep my thoughts from wandering, and bless to me this service. For Christ's sake.

Book of Prayers for Boys

O God, teach me to set aside the opinions of men and to begin to think fresh thoughts with you alone.

Geddes Macgregor

Almighty God, send thy Holy Spirit into my heart that I may attend to what I hear and mean what I say. Help me to join in the prayers truly and to remember that I am in the presence of God.

Daily Prayers for a Boy

Almighty God, unto whom all hearts be open, all desires known, and from whom no secrets are hid, cleanse the thoughts of our hearts by the inspiration of thy Holy Spirit, that we may perfectly love thee and worthily magnify thy holy name; through Jesus Christ our Lord.

Book of Common Prayer

Heavenly Father, we thank you for this church which is your house. Thank you for the people who worked hard to build it and for all those who have looked after it and who care for it today. Thank you for all the people who have worshipped you here through hundreds of years and for the times when we, too, meet here to worship you.

Hope Freeman

In Church

O Lord God, our Father, we thy children worshipping in thy house would be true worshippers and true givers. Make us strong to serve thee. Help us to face life with courage, to meet its difficulties with loyalty and steadfastness. We are very sure at this moment on whose side we want to be. Help us when the moment of testing comes that we may never turn our backs and run away. Help us to be conquerors, not cowards, real followers of the greatest of all hero-conquerors, Jesus Christ.

Doris W. Street

We thank you, Lord, that we can freely worship you. Help us, we pray, to continue our worship through the coming week by living lives which are filled with love, both for you and for all mankind.

Prayers for Today's Church

After Service

Pardon, O Lord, all my wandering thoughts and cold desires; and grant that what I have said with my lips I may believe in my heart; and what I believe in my heart I may show forth in my life, through Jesus Christ our Lord.

MORNING AND EVENING PRAYERS

O God, let me not interrupt you with my chatter. Let me listen, rather, to your still, small voice.

Geddes MacGregor

Heavenly Father, thank you for keeping me safe all through the night. Thank you for bringing me to a new day. Help me to bring to this day happiness and joy, friendliness and understanding, loyalty and courage, believing what you tell us – that you are with us always.

Ena V. Martin

Dear Heavenly Father, thank you for a night of rest. Thank you for the opportunity of facing another day. Whatever it may hold in store for me, whether it be joy or sorrow, may I always remember you are my constant companion.

Ena V. Martin

All through this day, O Lord, let me touch as many lives as possible for thee. And every life I touch, do thou by thy Holy Spirit quicken, whether through the word I speak, the prayer I breathe, or the life I live.

O God, help us to go about life eagerly today –
Save us from grudges

Save us from being grumpy,
Save us from thinking only of our own things.
What we have to do, let us do it with our whole hearts –
Our jobs about the house;
Our lessons at school;
Our games with others.

Rita Snowden

May I live this day for you, heavenly Father;
May I use rightly the gifts you have given me, and not throw
them away as if they were not worth having.
Take my mind, and keep it active in your service;
Take my heart, and keep it loving in your service;
Take my body, and keep it pure and healthy in your service.

Ena V. Martin

O God, our Father, help us all through this day so to live
that we may bring help to others, credit to ourselves and to
the name we bear, and joy to those who love us, and to thee.

Help us to be,
Cheerful when things go wrong;
Persevering when things are difficult;
Serene when things are irritating.

Enable us to be,
Helpful to those in difficulties;
Kind to those in need;
Sympathetic to those whose hearts are sore and sad.

Grant that,
Nothing may make us lose our temper;
Nothing may take away our joy;
Nothing may ruffle our peace;
Nothing may make us bitter towards any man.

So grant that all through this day all with whom we work, and all whom we meet, may see in us the reflection of the Master, whose we are, and whom we seek to serve. This we ask for thy love's sake.

William Barclay

O God, our Father, who dost desire us to love and to serve one another, and who hast created us for fellowship with thee and with our fellow men, grant unto us all through this day the gifts and the graces which will make us easy to live with. Grant us courtesy, that we may live every moment as if we were living at the court of the king.

Grant us tolerance, that we may not be so quick to condemn what we do not like and what we do not understand.

Grant us considerateness, that we may think of the feelings of others even more than of our own.

Grant unto us kindliness, that we may miss no opportunity to help, to cheer, to comfort and to encourage a brother man.

Grant unto us honesty, that our work may be our best, whether there is anyone to see it or not.

Grant unto us so to live this day that the world may be a happier place because we passed through it.

William Barclay

O Lord, we thank thee for this new day with its new strength and vigour, its new hopes and its new opportunities. Help us to meet its joys with praise, its difficulties with fortitude, its duties with fidelity. Grant us wisdom and clear vision. Direct our steps and guard us from error. And of thy great mercy deliver us from evil; through Jesus Christ our Lord.

H. Bisseker

Grant to us, O God, this day, to do whatever duty lies before us with cheerfulness, and sincerity of heart. Help us in all things fearlessly to do what we know to be right; save us from hypocrisy and pretence. Make us truthful, unselfish, and strong. And so bring us to the ending of the day unashamed, and with a quiet mind. We ask this through Jesus Christ our Lord.

Prayers for use in Hospitals

O God, I give myself to you. Use me to bring honour to your name today, that the world may honour you.

Young Christians at Prayer

O God, the Father of us all, who hast safely brought us to the beginning of another day, send thy blessing on all whom we shall meet, and let us do only what thou canst bless. Teach us to think much of our duties and little of our rights; make us to know that to love and be loved is better than great possessions; and help us to follow the example of our Saviour Christ and to be made like unto him.

Enter with us, O God our Saviour, upon the life of this day. Be thou our companion in all that we have to do. In our difficulties grant us guidance. In our weakness send us strength. Help us to do our duty earnestly, to bear our troubles bravely, and to serve thee and our fellows with wisdom, and with cheerfulness; through Jesus Christ our Lord.

H. Bisseker

Now another day is breaking,
Sleep was sweet and so is waking,
Dear Lord, I promised you last night

63

Never again to sulk or fight.
Such vows are easier to keep
When a child is sound asleep.
Today, O Lord, for your dear sake,
I'll try to keep them when awake.

Ogden Nash 1902–1971

O God, our Father, we thank thee for taking care of us so far in our lives, and for giving us so many good things to enjoy. Send us on our way now to do our duty through the day. Grant that we may always stand firm on the side of right, and spread thy kingdom of goodness and happiness wherever we go.

Lord, for tomorrow and its needs
    I do not pray
Keep me, my God, from stain of sin
    Just for today.

Let me both diligently work
    And duly pray
Let me be kind in word and deed
    Just for today.

So for tomorrow and its needs
    I do not pray
But keep me, guide me, love me, Lord
    Just for today.

R. C. Meyer

O God, our Father and our friend, we would thank thee for all the happiness of the day that has gone. We thank thee for all who have been specially kind to us today, who have helped us by their words, their sympathy or their example.

We thank thee for work honestly done and games well played; for friendship and fun, and for all other good things; through Jesus Christ our Lord.

Hugh Martin

Thank you, God, for our home, with its welcome at the end
   of the day. A lot of things have happened, and a lot of
   people have helped us today.
Parents and teachers, bus-drivers and play-mates;
People who kept the traffic flowing;
People who protected us from law-breakers,
Thank you for the fun we've had, for the chatter with friends,
   for the new things learned.
Forgive us if we've been cheeky.
Forgive us if we've been selfish
Forgive us if we've been untruthful.
We didn't mean to be like this – if we were – now we're sorry.
   Send us to our sleep forgiven, secure in your love and
   keeping; and waken us to a better day tomorrow.

Rita Snowden

O God, our Father, as we look back across this day, we ask thee to forgive us if today we have made things harder for others.

Forgive us if we have made work harder for others, by being careless, thoughtless, selfish and inconsiderate.

Forgive us if we have made faith harder for others, by laughing at things they hold precious or casting doubts on things they hold dear.

Forgive us if we have made goodness harder for others by setting them an example which would make it easier for them to go wrong.

Forgive us if we have made joy harder for others, by bringing gloom and depression through our grumbling discontent.

Forgive us, O God, for all the ugliness of our lives; and tomorrow help us to walk more nearly as our Master walked, that something of his grace and beauty may be on us. This we ask for thy love's sake.

William Barclay

O God, pitch your tent with me this night.

Geddes MacGregor

Provoke me, Lord, to do better tomorrow.

Geddes MacGregor

The good of today I thank you for,
The bad of today I am sorry for,
The world of today I pray for,
Lord, I am trying to trust you and love you,
I trust myself to you tonight.

Young Christians at Prayer

Be near me, Lord Jesus,
I ask you to stay
Close by me for ever,
And love me, I pray.

PRAYERS FOR RULERS
AND LEADERS

We ask you, O God, to give wisdom and understanding to our rulers and leaders. We pray not only for those who guide the affairs of this nation but for all who, throughout the world, have accepted the responsibility of government. Help them to exercise their powers without prejudice or self-interest, to be just and honest in all their duties, working only for that which is well-pleasing to you.

A PRAYER FOR BROWNIE-GUIDES

Dear Lord, we ask that you will bless Elizabeth, our Queen, in all the work she does for our country and for the Commonwealth of nations to which we belong. Be with her when she has to leave her home and family and make long journeys; help her when she has hard things to do.

May her statesmen rule us wisely, and may we, as Brownies, always try to be useful and helpful to all those we meet day by day.

Brownie-Guide Prayer Book

Almighty God, Lord of all, and King of kings, please bless our Queen as she seeks to serve you in the very special place in which you have put her. Help her to be wise in all her thoughts and ways, and give her patience and understanding

as she meets and talks with so many different people every
day.

Beryl Bye

O God,
King of kings, and Lord of lords,
We pray today for statesmen, leaders and rulers.
May they be quiet in spirit, clear in judgment,
Able to understand the issues that face them.
May they think often of the common people on whose behalf
    they must speak and act.
May they remember that in keeping thy laws is man's only
    good and happiness.
Grant them patience, grant them courage,
Grant them foresight and great faith.
In their anxieties be thou their security,
In their opportunities be thou their inspiration,
By their plans and their actions may thy kingdom come, thy
    will be done.

Lilian Cox

PRAYERS FOR PEACE

O God of peace, we give thanks
> For all thy servants who work for goodwill and understanding among men,
> For all men and women of past days who have walked the ways of peace.
> For those who are carrying the Gospel of the Prince of Peace to earth's farthest shores,

> For all those who this day are working and praying that wars may end and that understanding and sympathy may increase.
>> *A. Murray Smith*

O God, send thy Spirit into our hearts that we may hate war and love peace. Teach the children of our own and every land that it is better to love one another than to fight, so that war and bitterness may cease, and thy kingdom of love may be set up through all the world for the sake of Jesus Christ, our Lord.
> *Vivyen Bremner*

Please guide the leaders of many different countries at the meetings where they try, by working together, to make the world a better and a safer place.

Help them to want peace rather than power, and show them how they can share the food in the world so that no one need be hungry.
> *Beryl Bye*

O God, who in thy love, hast made all the nations of the world to be one family, help us all to love and understand one another. Take away hatred and bitterness, make war to cease so that all together we may work for the coming of thy kingdom and dwell in thy peace.

Evelyn Underhill

PRAYERS LINKED WITH
THE BIBLE

Dear God, thank you for the Bible in which we can read about your love. Thank you especially for the stories of Jesus and those which tell how much he loves us and cares for us. Thank you for sending Jesus to live like us, showing how much you love us.

Teach and help us to love you more and more every day and so to be more loving to others.

N.M.

Lord Jesus, we remember how, when you were born, there was no place in all the town of Bethlehem to lay a baby down. Take now into your loving care, all homeless children everywhere. And we remember how, at Galilee, the waiting crowd as by a miracle was fed, on two small fishes and five loaves of bread. Lord Jesus, listen to our prayer, feed hungry children everywhere.

Sally Cawley

O Lord Jesus Christ, who was found in the temple sitting at the feet of the teachers, help us this day in our school to follow thy example. Make us obedient to our teachers and attentive to our lessons, reverent before thee and kind to each other.

B.B.

Jesus! Thou didst the fishers call,
Who straightway at thy voice left all
To teach the world of thee;
May I with ready will obey
Thine inward call, and keep the way
Of thy simplicity.

F. W. Faber 1814–63

Lord, I am always running to you when I am distressed and in need, so now that everything is going well I would like to thank you for all you have done for me and for giving me so much joy. I also ask your forgiveness for the times I fail to thank you, like the healed lepers in the Gospel. Help me to bring all my life and its events to you so that I can share them with you and come to know and love you better.

Michael Hollings and Etta Gullick

Lord Jesus, we are thinking of you in the desert. We remember that for forty days and forty nights you were tempted there to disobey God's will. You know how often we are tempted to do wrong. Please show us how to overcome our temptations as you overcame your own. Help us to be strong-minded and teach us to banish wrong thoughts when they come. Make us true and brave and more like you every day.

Brenda Holloway

Loving Lord, who didst suffer so much for us, make us willing to deny ourselves for thee. As we remember the time of thy temptation in the wilderness, we pray that thou wilt give us the will-power to overcome all unworthy thoughts and deeds in our lives.

J. W. and S. Brimer

Lord Jesus, when you were in the wilderness you disciplined your body; you had the courage to resist temptation and the strength to take the way which led to the cross. Help us, O Lord, to follow your example, that we may be stronger in body and mind and so be ready and able to take our place in the world.

N.M.

Dear Lord, when you were on earth you found time to pray. Sometimes I find it so difficult to pray. There are days when I seem too busy or too tired. Did you ever feel like that? Help me to make time for prayer, and if, sometimes, it seems not to be effective, help me to know that you are listening and will answer in the way that is best for me. Help me, when I'm most doubting, to know that you are there.

N.M.

Dear Father, I wish I could be like Samuel and hear you speaking to me. When I say my prayers I never hear you answer. I never hear you call me to do something for you, or even say you've heard what I've said. Is it because I don't stop to listen?

N.M.

Lord God, I do not think that men, still less a child like me, will need to prove our faith, as Daniel did, inside a lion's den. Please give us all the strength to prove our faith in other ways; by being kind to everyone we meet, helpful to everyone in need. So may we show, dear Lord, throughout our days, our lasting love for you.

Sally Cawley

Jesus, the carpenter's son, teach us to judge work only by its value to thee. Teach us to seek prayerfully the work in which we are best fitted to serve thy kingdom and our fellow pilgrims. Then give us grace to labour steadfastly and with a sure content. Help us to see that talents are not merely great gifts of mind or body, but faith, humility, gentleness, patience, goodness and all the flowers and graces of the Spirit. Help us to know that none is born without value to thee and all have some talent that can be invested in thy love.

Accept, O Lord, our small talent, as thou accepted the widow's mite, and bless its use in thy service for thy honour and glory and the good of all mankind.

T.T.

O Almighty God, who hast appointed unto every man his work; give me grace to try and improve whatever talents thou hast committed to my trust and grant that whatever I do I may do it with all my might, to thy honour and glory, for Jesus Christ's sake.

O God, who hast commanded that no man should be idle, give us grace to employ all our talents and faculties in the service appointed for us; that, whatsoever our hand findeth to do, we may do it with our might.

James Martineau 1805–1900

Loving Heavenly Father,

I remember how Jesus showed his love when he was in this world;

I remember that he healed a boy who was ill, and that he hurried to a little dying girl:

I remember that he understood and cared about hungry people: and that he watched the children playing:

I remember that lovingly, he looked for those who had done wrong, and that he helped them to be good and happy again.

I know that you sent Jesus to help us to understand how you
love us.
Please love me too, like that; and help me to learn to love
other people in your way.

Ella Forsyth Wright

Lord Jesus, I have watched the sea when I have been to the
coast on holiday.
Even in summer, the waves pound the beach and hiss over
the shingle
As if they were living, angry things.

I have watched the sea on the television news in winter
When great breakers have pounded the promenades
And tossed cars about as if with a giant hand.

I'm always a bit afraid of the sea, Lord,
Even in its summer moods.

Yet you could stand erect in a heaving boat
And command the tumbling waves to be still.
No wonder your disciples were amazed.
What courage you showed!

Please share that courage with me, Lord Jesus.
Great waves of temptation beat against the shores of my heart.
Help me to still their storm,
And bring me to the safe harbour of your peace.

Mary Drewery

I was reminded of you today, Lord Jesus.

I was watching some sheep being prepared for an agricultural
show.
They were nervous, crowding to one end of their pen

As a young farm labourer tried to brush them down.
Then the farmer climbed into the pen and spoke to them.
It was wonderful to watch the effect on the sheep.
They stopped shivering and stood perfectly still;
They even let the farmer tidy up their fleece with his shears.

I thought of your words, Jesus: 'My sheep hear my voice'.
You knew what you were talking about, Lord,
When you likened yourself to a good shepherd.
Open my ears to recognise your voice when you speak to me,
    Lord Jesus.
Many people give me advice
But I can't always be sure it is right.
I get nervous like those sheep.
But when I hear your voice clearly above all others
I know I can trust it,
For you are my good shepherd, Lord.

Mary Drewery

Dear Lord Jesus, help us to have the courage of our convictions. We know what is right but sometimes we are afraid to stand up for it. You were never afraid of what people might say or think. You must have known it would offend the Pharisees when you healed the man on the sabbath day. When you drove the people out of the temple because they were using it as a market place, you knew you would be unpopular, but you were not afraid to do what was right. Help me to know what is right and to have the courage to do it, whatever it costs.

N.M.

Dear God, please make me like the Samaritan who saw someone in need and did what he could to help. Please God, don't let me be like those who didn't care and passed by without even thinking what they could do to help.

N.M.

Dear Lord Jesus, help me not to be like the self-righteous Pharisee, boasting that I am better than other people because I go to church and try to do the things that are right.

Please help me to be humble like the tax-collector and ask your forgiveness for all the things I have done wrong.

N.M.

O Jesus Christ, who didst see a poor woman give away more than she could afford, help us to remember that no part of our lives is too small or unimportant for you to notice and that you will use all that we have if we give it to you.

Dear God, I find it so hard to forgive those who are unkind to me, or who blame me for things which are not my fault. I go on bearing a grudge against them and even when they try to make it up I feel bitter and hard.

I know this is wrong. When Peter asked Jesus how many times he ought to forgive someone who had wronged him, Jesus said he must go on and on forgiving. Jesus even prayed for forgiveness for those who crucified him. Please help me to be more like him and be willing to forgive.

N.M.

Dear Lord, you have called us to be your witnesses. Please help us to be worthy of that calling; to have at least some of the virtues which show that we are your followers.

Please God help us never to deny that we are your disciples, as Peter did; but if we do fail, please forgive us and call us back again.

N.M.

PRAYERS FROM THE BIBLE

Lord, here is my Bible,
Here is this quiet room,
Here is this quiet time,
And here am I.
Open my eyes;
Open my mind;
Open my heart;
And speak.
                    Dick Williams

I will both lay me down in peace and sleep; for thou, Lord,
only makest me dwell in safety.
                    Psalm 4, verse 8

It is a good thing to give thanks unto the Lord, and to sing
praises unto thy name, O most high;
    To show forth thy loving-kindness in the morning, and thy
faithfulness every night.
                    Psalm 92, verses 1 and 2

O Lord, thou has searched me, and known me.
Thou knowest my down-sitting and mine uprising,
Thou understandest my thought afar off.
Search me, O God, and know my heart;
Try me, and know my thoughts:
And see if there be any wicked way in me,
And lead me in the way everlasting.
                    Psalm 139, verses 1 and 2; 23 and 24

78

Two things have I required of thee;
Remove far from me vanity and lies;
Give me neither poverty nor riches,
Feed me with food convenient for me;
Lest I be full and deny thee, and say,
'Who is the Lord?' or lest I be poor and steal,
And take the name of my God in vain.

Proverbs 30, verses 7, 8 and 9

THE CHRISTIAN LIFE

Lord Jesus, I don't know much about you,
But I am willing to learn;
And I am ready to give all that I know of myself
To all that I know of you;
And I am willing to go on learning.
Quoted by permission of Dr. Donald Coggan,

Our Father in heaven,
We pray thee to send into our hearts
and into the hearts of all men everywhere
the spirit of our Lord Jesus Christ.
John Oxenham 1853-1931

O Lord, our Father, thou has promised to hear thy children when they pray to thee. Help us now to pray, teach us what to ask for, help us to mean what we say, and give us grace to love thee more, and to love the people for whom we pray. For Jesus Christ's sake.

Selina Fitzherbert Fox

O God, we pray—
that thy love may rule in our hearts,
that thy truth may rule in our minds;

that thy presence may rule in our souls,
by the power of the Holy Spirit,
for Jesus' sake.
Father Andrew (adapted from singular to plural)

Put love into our hearts, Lord Jesus—
    love for you;
    love for those around us;
    love for all we find it hard to like.
                Ena V. Martin

Lord, I know
that one of the best ways I can show
my love for you is by loving other people.
Sometimes this is easy—
when I'm with people I like—

Please help me when loving is hard,
when people are unkind,
when they don't understand,
when I just don't like them.

Teach me to love as you loved
when you were walking about in Palestine—
Teach me to love as you love now—
Everyone
Always.
        Brother Kenneth and Sister Geraldine

A PRAYER FOR A BROWNIE-GUIDE
    Dear Father in heaven,
    We know we are your children,
    We want to serve you faithfully,
    We want to keep our Brownie Promise.

Help us to listen to your voice:
Help us to be willing and quick to do your work:
Help us to be friendly and loving:
And help us to thank you every day
For all your gifts to us.
Through Jesus Christ our Lord.

Brownie-Guide Prayer Book

O thou great Chief, light a candle within my heart that I
may see what is therein and sweep the rubbish from thy
dwelling-place.

Prayer of an African girl

By the prayers of Jesus, Lord teach us how to pray,
By the gifts of Jesus, Lord teach us how to give,
By the toils of Jesus, Lord teach us how to work,
By the love of Jesus, Lord teach us how to love,
By the cross of Jesus, Lord teach us how to live.

In Excelsis

Set a watch, O Lord, upon our tongue;
    that we may never speak the cruel word which is untrue;
    or being true, is not the whole truth;
    or, being wholly true, is merciless;
    for the love of Jesus Christ our Lord.

G. W. Briggs

Help us, O Lord, to recognise thy constant care of us as we
go through the week. Be with us in our homes that we may
take our full share of all that is to be done there; and may we
not forget to show our gratitude for what is done for us.

E.R.

O Lord Jesus Christ, look into my heart and see the good things there as well as the bad. You know that I really want to serve you and be the best that I can be. Help me to know that you love me always, even when I have done wrong. And help me, by your Spirit, to triumph over temptation and to be more worthy to follow you.

J. M. Macdougall Ferguson

Bless all those I shall meet today, and help us to help each other.

Ena V. Martin

As thou has lived for others,
So may we for others live;
Freely have thy gifts been granted,
Freely may thy servants give.
Thine the gold and thine the silver,
Thine the wealth of land and sea,
We the stewards of thy bounty
Held in solemn trust for thee.

Lord, make me the sort of person who causes other people to feel happier, whatever I feel like myself.

Young Christians at Prayer

That which is worth knowing
That which is worth hearing
That which is worth seeing
That which is worth believing
Give us grace to find.
Give us this day our daily bread.
May I work hard as one who needs not be ashamed.
Even today may I discipline myself to be careful and thorough.

Even today may I exert myself to the utmost of my ability.
Even today may I learn to seek after knowledge and truth.
Today and every day.

K. A. Clegg

God give us sympathy and sense,
And help me keep my courage high
God give me calm and confidence,
And, please—a twinkle in my eye.
Margaret Bailey

God, give me strength to run this race,
God, give me power to do the right,
And courage lasting through the fight;
God, give me strength to see thy face,
And heart to stand till evil cease,
And at the last, Oh God, thy peace.
Jane Vansittart

Lord, you know what it is to be tired, and concerned to get work finished. You know what it is to be waiting, cold and wet.

Give your strength to all who are fed up, and to me that I may do my work well.

Young Christians at Prayer

O God, you know the unexpected things which will come to challenge me this week. When the unexpected opportunity comes, in school, on the playing field, or at home, help me to meet it with quiet courage and daring. And if I may not have success in all that I do, give me the joy of knowing that I have done my best and the patience to try again, for Jesus' sake.

J. M. Macdougall Ferguson

O God, who made all things help us to live thoughtfully and kindly in thy world.

Teach us not to hurt or destroy or despoil the beauty of thy handiwork.

Teach us kindness to all that lives and to know the full value and meaning of life.

A. Murray Smith

Your beautiful world is being spoilt today, dear God, by our selfishness and greed. Instead of peace there is discord and war. Instead of love there is hatred and fear.

Help us, O Lord, to shut out of our individual lives all that is selfish and greedy, all hatred and bitterness. Help us to have love and forgiveness in our hearts; the desire to help others and to share the good things of life. Then, perhaps, if we learn to live generously and peaceably as individuals we shall become a generous and peaceful nation and other nations will follow our example.

N.M.

Help me, O God, to put away the fears of childhood;
 Fear of being alone, and of the dark;
 Fear of doing distasteful things, and hurting myself;
 Fear of strangers, going to fresh places, meeting people;
  doing unfamiliar things;
 Fear of failure.

Teach me rather, O God, to fear
 Compromising with the truth by silence or speech;
 Losing what good name I have;
 Bringing hurt or shame upon my family and friends;
 Breaking my word;
 Betraying Christ.

Leonard P. Barnett

O God, give us courage—courage to make experiments, and not to be afraid of making mistakes; courage to get up when we are down; courage to work with all our might for the coming of thy kingdom on earth; through Jesus Christ our Lord.

O Jesus Christ, strong son of God, friend of the weak, who dost lead thy servants into battle against disease and sin; make us brave in following thee; make us worthy of the hosts who have striven in thy name for right and freedom. Teach us to hate all oppression and kindle in our hearts a passion for justice and kindness. Make us ready to succour the weak, with hearts that sympathise and hands that help. Give us thine own courage that we may not falter in thy service, but be worthy of thee, our Captain.

Hugh Martin

O Lord, quicken in us the spirit of courage. We will go forth with hopeful minds to the duties and conditions of this day—confident that with your help we can fashion something good out of whatever material the day will provide.

Lord Jesus, please give us courage to keep on when things are difficult, faith when we must face pain or disappointment, and sympathy to speak to someone who is lonely or sad—thus may our lives show a little of your endless love.

Phyllis Lovelock

O Holy Spirit, grant us the gift of courage. Enable us to live as Jesus lived, in steadfast opposition to sin and in courageous faith in the power of God. As Jesus faced the hatred of enemies and the desertion of friends on earth, so may we be prepared to face manfully and with unfailing faith whatever opposition or enmity our service of Christ may arouse against us, in certain hope that in all things we can be strengthened through him who has overcome the world.

E. M. Venables

Grant us, O Lord,
in thought, faith;
in word, wisdom;
in deed, courage;
in life, service:
through Jesus Christ our Lord.
(Inscription on a column in front of the Viceroy's House in New Delhi)

O God of love, Father of us all, help us to banish from among us all jealousy, suspicion, quarrels and pride; give us the spirit of comradeship, and teach us the joy that lies in helping one another; enable us to take a pleasure in the success of others, to be generous of praise and slow to criticise; to frame our actions and thought in conformity with those we learn of him, in whom we all, though many, are called to be one body, even Jesus Christ our Lord.

Abbotsholme (1935) Prayer-Book

Fill our hearts, O Lord, with faith and love for thee and for one another. In all our dealings deliver us from mean suspicions and from unworthy thoughts, and let our minds be ready always to believe good rather than evil of one another. Save us from unkindness and selfishness, from caring only for ourselves and not for thee and for others. May we cherish in our hearts no desires which we cannot name to thee in our prayers, or ask thee readily to grant; but do thou keep us pure in mind and body for thy service.

Lord, we need your help.
We need a calm mind; grant us your peace.
We need a clear head; grant us your wisdom.
We need to be careful; grant us your patience.
We need to be inspired; grant us your enthusiasm.
Keep us from all panic as we put our trust in your power to
keep us this day.

K. A. Clegg

O God, we confess before thee all our sins—the words of
anger, the deeds of selfishness, the thoughts of hatred.
Yet we know thy love for us and pray that we may be
forgiven. As thou dost forgive us, help us to forgive each
other.

A. Murray Smith

Dear Father,
When we are tempted to be unkind,
When we are tempted to be unfair,
When to others' troubles we are blind,
Remind us how *we* would feel, and make us care.

Jack and Edna Young

Forgive us, O Christ, for all our wanderings.
Forgive us for not listening to thy voice calling us into
right ways.
Forgive us for our complaining and our worrying that have
made us lose our trust in thee.
Forgive us for anger and selfishness and for greed.
For all these we are sorry and pray that they may be taken
from us.

A. Murray Smith

Father,
I wish I hadn't behaved like that today.
I didn't really want to
But I couldn't stop myself.

There are two sides to me,
A good side and a bad side, and today
the bad was on top.

Please forgive me
I am truly sorry.
Help me to see my faults and to overcome them.

Help me, too, not to lash back when others hurt me.
Teach me to forgive them
and to treat them as friends.

Brother Kenneth and Sister Geraldine

Dear God, thank you for loving us. Please help us to love you more. Forgive us for all the wrong things we do. Help us to know what is right and to do it, however hard it is. We want to help you do your work but we don't know how. Show us what we can do to help others, then please give us the power and the will to do it.

O God, you made us and you love us, thank you for being so willing to forgive us. Make us quick to own up to you whenever we do wrong so that we may quickly be forgiven. Then our day will not be spoilt by worry and we can be happy all day long, through Jesus Christ our Lord.

Dick Williams

Lord Jesus Christ,
We confess to you now
The wrong things we have done,
The wrong words we have said,
The wrong in our hearts:
Please forgive us
And help us to live as you want us to.

Christopher Idle

O God,
we ask you to forgive us
for
      the things we have not thought about
      the jobs we have not done
      the words we have not spoken.

We ask you to help us
      to think
      and do
      and say
the right things at the right time.

Brother Kenneth and Sister Geraldine

Forgive us, Lord, when jealousy, greed, temper, pride, or indignation disturb the peace of our family. Help us to find the right words and the right actions to soothe and heal the hurt. Forgive us when we quarrel. Help us to forgive others: help others to forgive us; through Jesus Christ our Lord.

Patricia Mitchell

O God, who knowest how hard it often is for us to do right, help us to fight against the wrong. Help us to be brave when we are afraid; to be cheerful when we are disappointed; to be pleasant when we feel angry or sulky. Help us always to tell the truth even when it will bring trouble upon ourselves. O God, thou art strong and thou art loving. Help us, for Jesus' sake.

Elfreyda M. C. Wightman

Heavenly Father, help us to feel that thou art near us now when we are sad. Thou knowest, O Father, that it is hard for us to keep on trying to be good when things seem all to go wrong; but please help us to be brave and to be strong. Help us to remember in our trouble that thou art with us. Hear our prayer, O God, and keep us close to thee, for the sake of Jesus, thy Son, who hath told us of thy love.

Elfreyda M. C. Wightman

Lord, help us, as we travel the road of life, to reject the easy and tempting paths of laziness, greed and selfishness and by choosing the right way to use our time and abilities to help and cheer others; so passing on the love and help we ourselves have received on our journey.

Phyllis Lovelock

O God, our Father, so guide our lives, we pray, that in all our thinking and doing we may accomplish thy will.

Guide our minds that we may think those things that are pure and may hold fast to all that is true.

Guide our intentions that we may at all times and in all matters be honest.

Guide our actions that we may be just, full of compassion and great in mercy.

Guide our lives that we may in them show thy loveliness.

A. Murray Smith

Dear Father, guide us through this day. Maintain us in safety. Hold us in the faith. Increase our understanding. Deepen our affection for one another and unite us all in devotion to thee.

A. Murray Smith

Heavenly Father, we are all different, but you have made everyone, and you know what is easy and what is hard for each of us. Help us always to do our best, and when we fail, to try again; for Jesus' sake.

Brownie-Guide Prayer Book

When we have fought a good fight;
When we are flushed with victory;
When we are filled with the joy of living,
Or when serenity enfolds us;
When we are steadily doing our best;
When we are loving our neighbours and serving the
   community;
Then, O Lord God,
Search us even more deeply,
To see that we do not believe our happiness is due to our
   merits,
That we are not pinning our trust on what we are and what
   we do,
Instead of on you.
And then, O Lord,
Help us to face in advance the difficulties that the future is
   sure to hold
Relying for the hard future, as for the easy present,
Not on our own good qualities,
But on your inexhaustible power.

Lilian Cox

O God, pardon whatever has not been quite truthful in me, and make me more watchful for the time *to* come. Help me to guard against everything that is false, may I not exaggerate nor be satisfied with confessing half the truth, nor repeat what I am not certain is true. Help me to think, speak and act as in thy presence, remembering that to thee all hearts are open, and that from thee no secrets can be hid. I thank thee, Lord, for all the mercies and comforts of the day; make me to remember that everything I have comes from thee. To thy care I commit myself and all my relations and friends this night, for the sake of Jesus Christ.

Daily Prayers for a Boy

Keep me, O God, from smallness of mind,
Let me be big in thought, in word and in action.
Let me be finished for ever with fault-finding and self-love.
May I put away all pretending and meet everyone face to face
    without self-pity or deceit.
May I never be hasty in judging and may I always be generous.
Let me take time for all things.
Make me grow calm, peaceful and gentle.
Teach me to put into action my good desires.
Teach me to be straightforward and fearless.
Grant that I may realise
    that it is the little things of life
    that make difficulties and divisions
    and that in the big things of life we are one.
And, O Lord God, do not let me forget to be kind.
My God, make us all of one mind in the truth, and of one
    heart in love.

Everyday Prayer Book

Bestow thy gift of creation upon us, dear Father, so that we be creators also. Help us to spend our days creating that which is beautiful and good. Help us to know that no effort of ours is judged by thee as too humble, but that all we do for thee is received gladly by thee.

A. Murray Smith

We thank thee, our Father, that nothing is too small or weak for thy service, and that thy love includes everyone of us, however young, however helpless. May we find thy plan for our lives, and seek thy strength to fulfil it.

J. W. Brimer and S. Brimer

O Jesus Christ, who didst teach thy disciples to seek first the kingdom of God, help us in our daily lives to remember to put first things first, to think the thoughts that are worth thinking, to do the things that are worth doing, and not to please ourselves. Teach us that in forgetfulness of self, and in ministering to the needs of others, we may be servants for the kingdom of God.

Prayers for use in Hospitals

Show us, Father, *whom* we can help, *how* we can help, *when* we can help. May we not be discouraged if our help passes unnoticed. Keep up our enthusiasm.

Jack and Edna Young

Dear Christ, teach us how to be humble.

Teach us how to live as you did, respecting others however lowly, poor and unattractive they are.

Teach us to do the humblest tasks the way you did, in unhurried quietness of mind, not thinking that we are fitted for more exciting duties.

Teach us to see how unworthy we are of all the gifts that you have given us, and not to regard them as our right.

O Lord, may we see how small we are in comparison with you, and in realising this forget our self-importance, and serve you and our brothers in true humbleness of heart.

Etta Gullick

O Saviour, who set thy face to go to Jerusalem to thy Cross and Passion, help us, thy weak and wavering disciples, to be firm and resolute in doing those things that lie before us. Help us to overcome difficulties and to persevere in spite of failures. When we are weary and disheartened and ready to give in, fill us with fresh courage and strength, and keep us faithful to our work, for thy name's sake.

Prayer in use in St. Paul's School, Darjeeling

Loving giver of life, I would use my life to praise thee. Teach me to know when to give in, when to be strong, and when to hold back, that I may grow in the Spirit which will guide me into the way of peace.

Vivyen Bremner

O God, in whose holy kingdom there is nothing that worketh evil or maketh a lie, help us to guard our words, to keep our promises and to speak the truth; through Jesus Christ our Lord.

We believe, O Lord, that you have a plan for the world, and that we can play a part in it. Your wish is that all men should live together happily as brothers. Fill our hearts with joy and peace which will be infectious to all we meet this week.

Jack and Edna Young

95

O Lord, help us to be masters of ourselves, that we may be the servants of others; through Jesus Christ our Lord.

Help us, Father, to enjoy giving as well as getting. To enjoy serving others as much as being served.

Jack and Edna Young

O Lord God, we come to thee to offer ourselves, all we are and all we hope to be. Use us as thou wilt. All that we have has come from thee, and we bring thy gifts to thee again, so that thou mayest use them and us for thy purposes.

B.D.M.

Teach us, Lord, how to follow you,
    How to give help
    without expecting anything in return.

    How to stick up for what we believe
    even when others jeer at us;

    How to do your work in the world
    and not get tired of doing it.

    How to be *real* Christians,
    just because this is what you want us to be
    and not because we hope to be praised for it.

Brother Kenneth and Sister Geraldine

Lord Jesus, you have taught us that love is the fulfilling of the law. Teach us now what love really is, how much it costs, how far it leads, how deep it digs into our selfish selves. Then give us the courage and the generosity to accept what this means today and tomorrow and in the whole future way of our lives.

Michael Hollings

96

Our Father in heaven, you alone have created all things very wonderfully, and given to each of us the gift of life. Let us learn to love you and to love our neighbours more than our small selfish selves.

Phyllis Lovelock

O Lord, give us clean hands, clean words, and clean thoughts. Help us to stand for the hard right against the easy wrong. Save us from habits that harm. Teach us to work as hard and play as fair in thy sight alone as if all the world saw. Forgive us when we are unkind, and help us to forgive those who are unkind to us. Keep us ready to help others though at cost to ourselves. Send us chances to do a little good every day, and so to grow more like Christ.

William de Witt Hyde

O God, help us to carry out cheerfully our daily tasks, and to do the good that lies near at hand. Make us thoughtful of others and teach us the meaning of true brotherhood, and strengthen us to follow thee, through Jesus Christ our Lord.

Prayer for use in the Brotherhood of Scouts

Lord Jesus, our Master, we thank thee for the example thou hast left us of love and kindness to all men, even to those who hated and despised thee. Teach us, we pray thee, how we may follow in thy footsteps. Show us that cruelty, unkindness, and selfishness are not worthy of true men, and give us opportunities every day of serving one another in kindness, forbearance and love, for thy name's sake.

A. G. Pite

Help me, O Lord, to share with others the things that I have. May I never be selfish or possessive. Let me remember that all I have really belongs to you, and was given to me to use in the way that you would have me use your gifts.

Ena Martin

O God, the giver of all good things, help us to be ready to share our possessions with other people. Teach us to give gladly, with no thought of what we are going to receive in return. May we remember that Jesus gave everything he had, even his life, to save the world. If, sometimes, we have to give things that are very precious to us, help us to make the sacrifice cheerfully.

Brenda Holloway

PRAYERS FOR OTHERS

O God, make the door of this house wide enough to receive all who need human love and fellowship; narrow enough to shut out all envy, pride and strife.

Make its threshold smooth enough to be no stumbling-block to children, nor to straying feet, but rugged and strong enough to turn back the tempter's power. God make the door of this house the gateway to thine eternal kingdom.

Ruined St. Stephen's, Walbrook, London

Help me this day always to be ready to help others,
If any are afraid, help me to give them courage;
If any are hurt, help me to give them comfort;
If any are lonely, help me to give them friendship.

Ena V. Martin

Lord, give me skill in comfort's art,
That I may consecrated be, and set apart
        Unto a life of usefulness;
For heavy is the weight of ill in many a heart,
And comforters are needed much
        Of Christlike touch.

Help us, dear God our Father, to be kind and loving to those with whom we live. Give us the ability to see things from their point of view. Teach us to be more understanding

99

and tolerant of the opinions of others – those in our own homes and those we meet each day.

Lord Jesus, help us to be more loving in our homes. Make us thoughtful for others and help us to think of kind things to do. Keep us from grumbling and ill-temper and help us to be cheerful when things go wrong and our plans are upset. May we learn to love and understand each other and think of others before ourselves.

Graham Salmon

O Lord Jesus, on the cross you remembered your mother and your friends. Make our homes to be homes of love. Bless every relationship between all your people, so that our earthly love may be caught up in God's love and your kingdom seen in the homes of your people.

Canon Anson

Please God, bless all mothers everywhere; the mothers of:
    the little white children,
    the little brown children,
    the little black children,
    the little yellow children,
    the children who live in the hot lands,
    the children who live in the lands of ice and snow.
Wherever there are mothers, please give them your blessing, dear God.

Vera Pewtress

Lord, didn't you come to heal our divisions?
Then help us to work with you, Lord,
Even with your people who are different from us.

Dear God, our Father, we know you love everybody all over the world. Please bless all the people who have come from other countries to live in our towns and villages. Help them to understand our language and to live happily with us. Make us willing to be understanding, friendly and helpful to them so that we may all live peacefully and happily together. We ask this for Jesus' sake, who taught us to love our neighbours as ourselves.

N.M.

Holy Father, we pray for the people in other lands, especially for the boys and girls.
Some would learn, but have no teacher;
Some are sick, and have no doctor;
Some are sad and have no one to comfort them;
Some are hungry and poor and have no helper;
Some are happy and cared for as we are ourselves,
For all we ask your loving care.
Supply their needs and comfort their hearts,
  through Jesus Christ, our Lord.

Heavenly Father, we pray for those who have gone to other countries with good news of Jesus.
When their work is difficult and tiring make them strong;
When they are lonely and homesick remind them that you are with them; when they are uncertain what to do, guide them, and keep them at all times loving you, for Jesus' sake.

M. H Botting

Bless, O Lord, all those who work without ceasing to send thy word to all lands and all peoples. To those who translate and print the Bible give patience and strength, and to the modern missionaries who still seek to teach the people to understand it, give courage and grace, for Jesus Christ's sake.

J. W. Brimer and S. Brimer

Dear God, we thank you for the modern inventions that are helping people to spread the good news of Jesus: for the radio messages going out into countries where missionaries are not allowed, for the aeroplanes keeping in touch with people in faraway places, for printing presses that turn out millions of booklets about Jesus; for new medicines and farm machinery. Please be with all those who use these new ways to reach even more people for you.

Zinnia Bryan

Lord Jesus, when you were on earth, they brought the sick to you and you healed them all. Today we ask you to bless all those in sickness in weakness and in pain:

those who are blind and who cannot see the light of the sun, the beauty of the world, or the faces of their friends;

those who are deaf and cannot hear the voices which speak to them;

those who are helpless and who must lie in bed while others go out and in:

Bless all such.

Those whose minds have lost their reason;

those who are so nervous that they cannot cope with life; those who worry about everything;

Bless all such.

Those who must face life under some handicap;

those whose weakness means that they must always be careful;

those who are lame and maimed and cannot enter into any of the strenuous activities or pleasures of life;

those who have been crippled by accident, or by illness, or who were born with a weakness of body or mind;

Bless all such.

Grant that we, in our health and our strength, may never find those who are weak and handicapped a nuisance, but grant that we may always do and give all that we can to help them and to make life easier for them.

William Barclay

Dear Father God, today we are remembering in our prayers all those boys and girls who cannot run and play as freely as we can.

We think about children who spend a lot of time in wheel-chairs, or lying in bed, or perhaps sitting by a window, watching their friends at play.

Help us not to be selfish; to spare time for them; to share our books, our records and our games, to tell our news and write happy letters.

Help boys and girls who are shut in at home, or in hospital, away from the streets and the fields, to know that we think about them and that people care for them.

May they find joy in pictures, and in music, in stories and in the friendship of others.

Jean Stevens

Lord, we thank you that we can hear the everyday sounds;

Music and the voices of our friends, radio and television, the fire alarm or the car coming round the corner that warns of danger.

Help us to be considerate to the deaf who often feel alone, cut off from these sounds. Let us talk to them clearly so that they may feel less isolated. And please give patience to those who teach them.

Phyllis Lovelock

Let us remember those whose lives are specially hard.

> For the blind, who miss the joy of seeing the lovely world around us;
> *Hear our prayer, O Lord.*
> For the deaf, who hear no music, nor the friendly sound of voices;
> *Hear our prayer, O Lord.*
> For the lame, who cannot share the delights of swift and lively movement;
> *Hear our prayer, O Lord.*
> For the sick in mind, who cannot know the pleasure of books and learning;
> *Hear our prayer, O Lord.*
> For the unwanted and neglected, who live in places where there is no love;
> *Hear our prayer, O Lord.*
> For the lonely, who feel that everyone is passing them by;
> *Hear our prayer, O Lord.*

Brownie-Guide Prayer Book

O God, we ask thy blessing on those who cannot see the beauties of nature or hear the sounds of life. Help them to feel thy presence. Guide their hands and feet in safety. Help them to find the gifts which thou hast given them instead of sight and hearing, so that they may use them to thy glory, for the sake of him who healed the blind and the deaf, Jesus Christ our Lord.

B.B.

Dear Father, we pray for all old people and those who feel that they are no longer needed. Comfort those who are ill, or tired, or lonely. Make us thoughtful and gentle when we speak to them, and show us how to help them; for Jesus' sake.

Brownie-Guide Prayer Book

O God, I remember before you those on whom at this time disaster has come.

Bless those whose loved ones have been killed, and those whose loved ones lost their lives in seeking to save the lives of others.

Bless those who have lost their homes, those who have seen all that they toiled for for a lifetime to build up, lost in an hour. Help us always to remember those whose job it is to risk their lives to rescue others or to keep them safe —those in the fire service, in the police, in the medical service. We shall forget this disaster, but we ask you always to remember those who will never forget, because life for them can never again be the same. This we ask for your love's sake.

William Barclay

Father God, I don't understand why you allow so many dreadful things to happen. I've puzzled over it but I can't find an answer. Is the next life going to be especially good for the innocent victims of disasters in this life? Perhaps it is. I hope so.

Please God, whatever happens, never let me turn away from you or stop believing you are a loving Father.

N.M.

If any life of mine may ease
The burden of another,
God give me love and care and strength
To help my ailing brother.

O God, who art the Father of us all, we pray for those homes where there is unhappiness. We pray for those girls and boys who spoil their homes by being selfish. We pray for those homes where there is hunger, want, sickness or sorrow,

and we ask thee to send thy blessing and a sense of thy love.
For Christ's sake.

O God, our loving father, we pray for the unhappy people
of many lands. We think of all those who have lost their
homes and their work; those who are ill and hungry; the
friendless and lonely who have had to leave their country.
May our prayers help to give them fresh courage. We ask this
for Jesus' sake.

Brownie-Guide Prayer Book

O God, we pray for all prisoners and wrong-doers. Help
them, O God, to seek forgiveness and a better way of life.
May this time of enforced absence be used as an opportunity
to find the way you want them to live and give them the will
and the courage to accept their punishment and do whatever is possible to make amends for the harm they have
done.

For their relations and friends who suffer shame and dis-
grace and hardship we pray thy blessing. We pray, too, for
those whose lives have been spoilt by law-breakers. Give us
all a true understanding of your love for all people, whatever
their circumstances and way of living, and teach us all your
way of forgiveness. For Jesus' sake we ask it.

N.M.

Dear Father, I pray today . . .

For the doctors who have learned to make sick people
better and to take away pain.

For the nurses and ambulance men whose arms and feet
often ache because they spend so many hours of the day and
night hurrying from bed to bed and looking after people who
cannot look after themselves.

For the specially trained men and women who show such patience in teaching damaged legs to walk again and helping hurt muscles to work again.

For the cleaners and cooks in hospitals who cheerfully work at the ordinary and uninteresting jobs so that the buildings are warm and clean and comfortable and the sick people have the right kind of food to make them well and strong again.

For all these people we pray and ask your blessing.

Beryl Bye

Give perseverance to all those who give up their lives to discover new medicines, drugs or treatments to help those who suffer. May they never be short of money or support to carry out their work, and grant to them wisdom and determination to go on and on.

Ena V. Martin

God our Father, whose son, Jesus Christ, loved to bring health and healing to those who were ill, may the Holy Spirit help and teach all doctors so that they try to find out more and more about curing and preventing illness. And help them, too, always to do their work lovingly and patiently even when they are very tired, just as Jesus did. Father, hear our prayer for his sake.

Hope Freeman

Bless, O God, all who are making discoveries in nuclear power, and put peace into their hearts. Let the great power that man is able to control today not be used to destroy all that you have made in your image and beauty.

Ena V. Martin

Lord Jesus, help all those who are working in the fields and factories and mines; sailors and fisherfolk, all who serve and labour. Help those whose work is very dull, the ones whose work is dirty and dangerous; and help Christian people to think and care about good conditions of work. Grant that employers and workers may understand each other and knit them all in one way of service; through thine own labour on earth.

Margaret Cropper

Heavenly Father, I would remember and give thanks for all the people who have worked to supply my food—those in my home; the people in far-away lands; on tea, or on coffee plantations; or on fruit farms; those who load the ships; the merchantmen who bring the ships safely to harbour; the workers in our own land. Bless them all, I pray.

Ella Forsyth Wright

Let us think of all the people who work for us:

The men and women in factories, shops, and offices,
Bless them and help them, O Lord.

The miners, fishermen, and all whose work is difficult or dangerous:
Bless them and help them, O Lord.

The farm workers, gardeners, builders, and all who help to provide our homes and food and clothing:
Bless them and help them, O Lord.

Those who carry people and goods, by road, railway, sea, or air:
Bless them and help them, O Lord.

The police, firemen, soldiers, sailors, and airmen, who
protect us:
Bless them and help them, O Lord.

The scientists, doctors, nurses, and hospital workers, who
care for our bodies:
Bless them and help them, O Lord.

The artists, entertainers, musicians, and writers, who
delight and instruct our minds:
Bless them and help them, O Lord.

Those who teach, govern, and guide us;
Bless them and help them, O Lord.

Those who can find no work to do:
Bless them and help them, O Lord.

Blessed Lord, who worked as a carpenter at Nazareth, teach
all people to work together for the good of the world and the
glory of God.

Brownie-Guide Prayer Book

Dear Lord Jesus, who did not fear the sea, guard all fishermen and sea-going people. If danger comes help them to be
calm and courageous and be with the people who answer their
call for help.

Give clear vision to Coastguards and Lighthouse Keepers
that they may quickly heed all calls from people in difficulty
or danger.

Give courage and strength to the brave men who man the
lifeboats in response to calls for rescue.

Help them all to feel the power of your presence and calm
the fears of relatives and friends of those in danger on the
sea.

N.M.

Lord, who hast made the earth, the air, the sky and the sea, we pray thee bless the work of all men at this time; grant that by the labour of the farmer and all who, under thy care, prepare the earth and sow the seed, there may be food in plenty for us this year, and that the corn may grow through rain and sunshine to a bountiful harvest.

M.C.

We thank you, Heavenly Father, for all the opportunities which will be ours during this week. We thank you for the people who will serve us in the shop and office and classroom. We thank you for those who make our lives brighter—the postman and the friendly neighbour. We thank you for those who make our lives easier—the dustman and the policeman. As people do so much for us, help us not to make their work a burden but rather look for ways in which we may help others too: for Jesus Christ's sake.

Ian D. Bunting

Hear our humble prayer, O God, for our friends the animals. We entreat for them all thy mercy and pity, and for those who deal with them we ask a heart of compassion, gentle hands and kindly words. Make us ourselves to be true friends to animals and so to share the blessing of the merciful. For the sake of thy son, the tender-hearted Jesus Christ our Lord.

Russian prayer

Great Father in heaven, thank you, for making animals to be our friends. Give us pity for all sick animals, for hunted and caged animals, for animals that are ill-treated and teased, and for any that are lost and frightened. Make us brave to defend any animal when we see it being cruelly treated. May we be the friends of all dumb creatures and save us from causing them any suffering through our own thoughtlessness.

Brenda Holloway

Heavenly Father, this has been a busy day—we haven't had many chances to sit quietly and think;

We want to sit quietly now, in your presence.

We are not afraid to do this, because we know you love us;

We know that all we have enjoyed today has come from you;

We know that you have used parents and teachers and bus-drivers and shop-keepers;

We know that you have kept us safe through the care of traffic-directors;

We know that you have provided us with food, through farmers and merchants and mothers and fathers.

We want to express our gratitude, before we prepare for bed, and slip into sleep.

We want to give ourselves, and all whom we love, over into your keeping this night. With our love.

Rita Snowden

PRAYERS FOR YOUNG PEOPLE

O Lord, open my heart that I may hear thy voice; show me thy will, O God, and give me grace to follow it for ever.

Malcolm L. Playfoot

O Lord, help me to understand that you ain't gwine to let nothin' come my way that you and me together can't handle.

Written by a negro boy who was running a losing race

Give us a sense of humour, Lord, and also things to laugh about. Give us the grace to take a joke against ourselves, and to see the funny side of the things we do. Save us from annoyance, bad temper, resentfulness against our friends. Help us to laugh even in the face of trouble. Fill our minds with the love of Jesus, for his name's sake.

A. G. Bullivant

Lord, you obviously enjoyed the business of being alive and enjoyed the ordinary things of life—
    your stories are full of them,
    and full of the beauty of the world too.

Lord, accept my laughter, my efforts to sing or whistle, my friendships, as an offering of thanksgiving.
    I'm glad to be alive,
    I'm glad there's so much to make life worth living.

C.E.M.

Dear Heavenly Father, I've been trying to pray, but my thoughts have been wandering again. When these thoughts have been bad please forgive me. When they have been good, consecrate them and lead me so that I may begin to think your thoughts after you and know that I am hearing your voice speaking to me in the stillness of this moment.

Graham Salmon

Lord, praying is not very easy,
Most of the time I'm busy
Working or enjoying myself.
I seem to cope with life quite well.
But then—out of the blue everything goes wrong.
I fall out with my best friend or one of the family becomes ill.
I feel so alone and life becomes meaningless.
Lord, you must have puzzled over all the misunderstandings
    between human beings; all the needless suffering in the
    world. Lord you learned to cope and managed to weather
    through.
Lord, you helped others to cope too.
Lord will you help me?

C.E.M.

Lord, we don't know very well how to talk to you, or how to listen. We don't even know just how this conversation works. But we know that you are with us and that you take the thoughts that are in our hearts and make them into the prayer that we ought to have said. Lord, help us to discover what you are like and what we are like so that we can know how to talk to you and how to listen.

C.E.M.

Dear God, I do know how fortunate I am; I could not ask for more. I have a loving family, a lovely home; I am happy at school, I have lots of friends, and yet I can still be unkind and selfish, and bad tempered. I forget to pray and gradually I drift further and further away from you. It is only now, having struggled to be good for so long by myself, having gone round and round in circles, never achieving anything, it is only now that I have suddenly realised how much I need you, and this is why you are there. Now I realise how important it is that you are always ready to forgive me. Please forgive me now.

God how could I have forgotten you again when there is everything to remind me? How can I walk out under your sky and not remember you? Help me, please, to discipline myself, so that I don't forget to pray. Help me to make time just to kneel down humbly and be quiet, and alone with you. A few more minutes to pray each night would do me far more good than a few more minutes sleep. Help me, please God, for why should I be so bad-tempered when I have nothing to worry about, and everything to be happy for?

Virginia Salmon

Lord, help those who thoughtlessly destroy.

That telephone kiosk—put there so that we can ring up our friends, call the garage when the car's broken down. Send for the doctor when there's been an accident.

But—NO—someone has damaged the phone.

Lord, help those who thoughtlessly destroy, to learn self control and to use their energy and ability creatively.

Phyllis Lovelock

O God, we go through life so lonely, needing what other people can give us, yet ashamed to show that need.

And other people go through life so lonely, hungering for what it would be such a joy for us to give.

Dear God, please bring us together, the people who need each other, who can help each other, and would so enjoy each other.

Marjorie Holmes

Give me the ability to see good in unexpected places
And talents in unexpected people
And give me, O Lord, the grace to tell them so.

Lord, growing up is bewildering and wonderful too. I long for something or someone but I don't know for what or for whom. This longing is painful but I sense that it is possible to attain to something which is beyond all dreams. There are so many things I'd like to do. I rush to do them, but then become afraid that the achieving will be disappointing, less than the striving and dreaming. Lord, give me courage to go on searching, don't let me become disillusioned; help me to find someone whose love will fulfil me and whom I will fulfil. Always be with me in my searchings and my findings, and let me see you in the midst of them.

Michael Hollings and Etta Gullick

Good Lord, help me to win if I may and if I may not make me a good loser.

Dear Lord Jesus, you taught your disciples that with God all things are possible. Give us a deeper sense of your presence that we may have the power to do what you are calling us to do.

O God, give me grace for this day.
Not for a lifetime, nor for next week, not for tomorrow, but
for today.
Direct my thoughts and bless them.
Direct my work and bless it.
Direct the things I say, and give them blessing too.
Direct and bless everything I think and speak and do
So that for this one day, just this one day, I have the gift of
grace that comes from your presence.
Oh God, for this day, just this one day, let me live
generously, kindly, in a state of grace and goodness
that denies my many imperfections and makes me
more like you.

Marjorie Holmes

We beseech thee, O God, the God of truth,
That what we know not of things we ought to know
Thou wilt teach us.
That what we know of truth
Thou wilt keep us therein.
That what we are mistaken in, as men must be,
Thou wilt correct.
That at whatsoever truths we stumble
Thou wilt yet establish us,
And from all things that are false
And from knowledge that would be hurtful,
Thou wilt evermore deliver us,
Through Jesus Christ our Lord.

Used in a service at the Church of St. Bride,
Fleet Street, London

Lord, help me to remember that all time belongs to you,
and that I am responsible to you for my use of it. Help me
neither to waste time nor be so obsessed with saving it that

I become the slave of time and lose my sense of proportion and values.

Lord, teach me to use my time to your glory, creatively, re-creatively, in that rhythm of involvement in the world and of withdrawal from the world which is your will for me. Save me both from running away from the world into self-centred religiosity and from running away from the inner life into compulsive busyness.

Lord, help me to live each day so that at the end of it there is nothing I cannot share with you, nothing for which I cannot thank you.

Margaret Dewey

Lord, increase our faith, that feeling towards thee as children we may trust where we cannot see, and hope where all seems doubtful, ever looking unto thee as our Father that ordereth all things well, and patiently doing the work thou hast given us to do; according to the word of thy Son, Jesus Christ our Lord.

George Dawson 1821-1870

We pray, heavenly Father, that we shall this and every day do thy will. We pray that we shall be patient and kind. We pray that we shall not be envious or conceited. We pray that we shall not be easily provoked and that we shall think no evil. We pray that we shall take pleasure not in wrong things but in the good and true.

A. Murray Smith

O Lord, who leadest us by ways we know not, through joys and sorrows, victories and defeats beyond our understanding, give us grace so to see thy guiding hand in all things that being neither lifted up by seeming success nor cast down by seeming failure, we may press forward where thou leadest, through Jesus Christ, our Lord.

From lack of reverence for truth and beauty, and being
contented with the mean and ugly:
  O God, deliver us.
From cowardice that dare not face new truth, the laziness
content with half-truths, and the arrogance that thinks it
knows all truths:
  O God, deliver us.
From all that is artificial in life, from all that is hollow or
insincere:
  O God, deliver us.
From trivial ideals and cheap pleasures:
  O God, deliver us.
From mistaking coarseness and vulgarity for humour:
  O God, deliver us.
From being rude, offensive, and ill-mannered:
  O God, deliver us.
From all uncleanness, unwholesomeness, and slackness:
  O God, deliver us.
From false piety that cannot laugh:
  O God, deliver us.
From the disloyalty of being satisfied with things as they are,
in the church and in the world, and from failing to share
thine indignation:
  O God, deliver us.

Youth at Worship

O Saviour Christ, we beseech thee, when the wind is
boisterous, and our faith weak, and we begin to sink even as
we would fain come to thee on the water, stretch forth thy
hand, O Lord, as of old to thy fearful disciple, and say to
the sea of our difficulties, 'Peace be still,' for thy holy name's
sake.

Dean Vaughan

Give me a quiet mind, O God, that I may worship thee with an undivided heart, and grant that in sincerity I may offer thee an acceptable service.

Malcolm L. Playfoot

Give me a good digestion, Lord,
And also something to digest;
But when and how that something comes
I leave to thee, who knowest best.

Give me a healthy body, Lord;
Give me the sense to keep it so;
Also a heart that is not bored
Whatever work I have to do.

Give me a healthy mind, Good Lord,
That finds the good that dodges sight;
And seeing sin, is not appalled,
But seeks a way to put it right.

Give me a point of view, Good Lord,
Let me know what it is, and why,
Don't let me worry overmuch
About the thing that's known as 'I'.

Give me a sense of humour, Lord,
Give me the power to see a joke,
To get some happiness from life,
And pass it on to other folk.

*Refectory Grace, Chester Cathedral
(Written by Thomas Harry Basil Webb when a
boy at Winchester. As a subaltern in the Welsh
Guards, he was killed in the First World War)*

Father, take all the broken bits of our lives
Our broken promises;
Our broken relationships;
Our differences of opinion,
Our different backgrounds, and shapes and sizes,
And arrange them together
Fitting them into each other to make something beautiful
Like an artist makes a stained glass window.
Make a design
Your design
Even when all we can see are the broken bits.

I see white and black, Lord,
I see white teeth in a black face.
I see black eyes in a white face.
Help me to see persons, Jesus—not a black person
or a white person, a red person or a yellow person,
but human persons.

Malcolm Boyd

O God, whose son, Jesus Christ, wrought as a craftsman amongst the sons of men, we ask thy blessing on all the toiling thousands of our cities. Grant to those who employ them a sense of justice and sympathy, and to those who labour a knowledge of the dignity and worth of their work. Keep us from prejudice of class or education and help us to bring about a brotherhood of men so that all may work gladly to build a city where slums are no more, oppression has ceased, competition is fair, and thou mayest ever be glorified in praise and worship and work, through Jesus Christ our Lord.

Youth at Worship

Lord, we acknowledge the deep divisions which exist in industry, the lack of understanding and suspicion and enmity between nations and groups, within trades, professions and vocations; the desperation and the greed which tempt men to violence; the privilege and pride of the strong, and the envy and resentment of the weak. Awaken in men's hearts the spirit of understanding, of forgiveness and hope for a better order, that we, no longer distrusting one another, may be taught the things which belong to our peace; through Jesus Christ our Lord.

B.K.

Our Father, I think of all the pain and heartache, the tears and sorrow, the greed and cruelty unloosed around the world. Help me to be an instrument of thine to alleviate the pain by this day:
    returning good for evil,
    returning soft answers for sharp criticisms,
    being polite when I receive rudeness,
    being understanding when I am confronted by ignorance
        and stupidity.
So may I, in gentleness and love, check the hasty answer, choke back the unkind retort, and thus short-circuit some of the bitterness and unkindness that has overflowed thy world. I ask this in the name of Jesus, who alone can give me the grace so to act.

Peter Marshall

Lord, we thank you for the advance of medical knowledge and the drugs to relieve suffering. Make us strong to resist the temptation to use these drugs wrongly lest we harm our healthy bodies or minds, and find ourselves unfit to enjoy your blessings.

For those who have yielded, we pray they may be helped to overcome their craving and learn to live anew.

Phyllis Lovelock

I will not hurry through this day!
Lord, I will listen by the way,
To humming bees and singing birds,
To speaking trees and friendly words;
And for the moments in between
Seek glimpses of thy great Unseen.

I will not hurry through this day;
I will take time to think and pray;
I will look up into the sky,
Where fleecy clouds and swallows fly:
And somewhere in the day, may be
I will catch whispers, Lord, from thee!

Ralph Spaulding Cushman

Lord, assist those who cannot find work, and all those who are in any way insecure. Send people to help and strengthen them, but best of all help them to solve their own problems. Show us how we can be of use, for so many restrictions seem to hinder us. Often we are afraid to become involved as we want to preserve our time or money for ourselves. Give us a persistent kind of love so that we will find a way to help, whatever the difficulties.

Michael Hollings and Etta Gullick

Father, we deplore that in so rich a world we tolerate poverty so harsh that men and women are embittered by it, and children die or survive, deprived in body, mind and spirit. Forgive our ignorance, our indifference, and our unwillingness to give the right priority to this responsibility. As we have the knowledge by which we can produce more than we need, stir up the compassion of us all by all means possible, and give us the will and the wisdom, that through political decisions, trade agreements, and personal service, we may find the way to share the wealth of the world, for the sake of him who was prepared to become poor that we might be rich, Jesus Christ our Lord.

B.K.

Father of all men, we pray for all those who in these days cannot find work by which to live; for all homes where there is want and poverty; for all those who are hungry and ill-clad, and especially for all little children. Stir up the conscience of this people, till this shame be removed from our land; for Jesus Christ's sake.

Open my eyes and my ears, O Lord my God, that I may see and hear more clearly the loveliness that thou has put into the world, and give me grace, I pray thee, to show in my turn some of thy gifts in my life, to thy glory.

Malcolm L. Playfoot

Almighty and everlasting God, who didst send thine only son, Jesus Christ, to be the saviour and healer of men, bless the work of all hospitals and medical missions. Help all ministers of healing to have ever present in their minds the example of our Lord, and his tenderness and sympathy faithfully to fulfil their holy calling, and crown their work with success and happiness. We commend, O God, all sufferers to thy loving care; soothe their pain, relieve their anxiety, help them to cast all their care upon thee, and to know that underneath are the everlasting arms.

Adapted from a prayer in use at the London Hospital

God, who hast made all creatures for thy own glory, and has continued all the things of this world for the service of mankind, bless, we pray thee, this machine built for our travel, that it may serve—without loss or danger—for spreading ever more widely the praise and glory of thy name, and for the quicker despatch of the world's affairs; and may foster in the hearts of those who travel in it a yearning for the things above, through Christ our Lord.

Prayer displayed in Aer Lingus passenger planes

God, make me single and sincere; take away all that is not true, all that hinders thy work in me; for only so shall I serve thee.

Malcolm L. Playfoot

Let thy love be my love, O Christ; may I see with the eyes that thou hast opened. Take away all jealousy and unkindness, all hardness and intolerance, that in simple and quiet service I may best please thee.

Malcolm L. Playfoot

Give us courage, O Lord, to stand up and be counted,
to stand up for those who cannot stand up for themselves,
to stand up for ourselves when it is needful for us to do so.
Let us fear nothing more than we fear thee.
Let us love nothing more than we love thee, for thus we shall fear nothing also.
Let us have no other God before thee, whether nation or party or state or church. Let us seek no other peace but the peace which is thine, and make us its instruments, opening

our eyes and our ears and our hearts, so that we should know
always what work of peace we may do for thee.

Alan Paton

Lord Jesus, you explained to your friends
That all this wonderful world in which we live
Is just like one room in a father's house.
You said there were other rooms, too,
And that you were getting them ready for us all,
And that one day you'd welcome us there.

I know that they wanted to know, God,
What those other rooms would be like;
I want to know, too.
But nobody knows;
You're keeping it as your surprise for us,
And because God is my loving Father
I know it will be a wonderful surprise,
And everything there, in that other room of yours,
Will be better than anyone can possibly imagine.

Some people have guessed
It might be like living in a city with streets of gold.
Some people have gussed there may be music and singing
More lovely than any heard here.
Some tired people have guessed
It will be a perfect rest.
But these are just guesses, God;
It's your secret. Your surprise.

So I'm glad, dear God,
That no one need be frightened about dying.
It will be just going to you
And to the place you have got ready for us;
Your most wonderful secret surprise.

Lilian Cox

Personal Prayers

Dear God, I feel so frightened,
I've got butterflies in my stomach.
My head feels like lead and I can't
    remember a thing.

People keep saying 'It's only an exam'
    as if it didn't matter.
Maybe it won't in the long run
But right here and now it's important.
So much hangs on the result
And I'm terrified lest I make a mess
    of the papers.

Everyone tells me that I have worked
    consistently and that of course
    I shall be all right.
But, Lord, I'm not so sure.
Suppose I haven't worked as hard as I should?
Suppose I've revised the wrong topics?
Suppose I've been deluding myself all the time?

Lord, reassure me of your presence.
Calm my jumping nerves.
Grant me your peace in the midst of
    all my turmoil.

I'm not asking for a miracle, Lord.
Just for the strength to do the best I can.
Help me to stave off the sudden rush
    of blood to the brain,
    the fit of nerves,
    the awful panic.
Enable me to think before I write,
    to write coherently, to answer the question.

Help me, Lord, to give of the best
   that is in me.

John E. Pugh Smith

O God, we start exams tomorrow. I've studied hard but I'm sure I haven't learned enough, and I cannot always remember what I've learned.

Please help me to keep calm and not be worried, so that I'll remember what I've learned and do my best. Then, even if I fail I need not be ashamed, and if I pass, please help me not to boast, but give my thanks to you for helping me to use the gifts which you have given. Thank you, God.

N.M.

Dear God, exams are finished and although I don't know if I've passed, I know I did my best. I asked for guidance, Lord, before I wrote a word, and got my confidence from you. So now, if I've passed, I want to thank you Lord, but if I've failed, I mean to take it well and try again next time.

N.M.

Lord, I believe that thou indeed hearest my prayer, and hearing, answerest. Help thou mine unbelief and my unwillingness to come to thee in prayer. Though my faith is so weak, yet do thou receive my petitions that I make in thine own name, Jesus Christ our Lord.

Malcolm L. Playfoot

Dear Father God, I know that I am in your care and that you love me, just as my own father does. You know all my joys and all the times when I am sad and unhappy.

Help me to trust you more and to know that you will be with me whatever happens, giving me whatever strength and courage I need to face the battles and temptations of life unafraid.

N.M.

Dear Father, we've been having careers talks at school and I'm still not sure what I want to do.

Please help me to choose the right job so that I can be happy in my work and be of use to others.

N.M.

What is the work you would have me do, Lord? Please guide me that I may find a job which is worth doing so that I may live full of purpose and joy in serving you, my creator, and helping in this world, whether it be in small ways or with wider responsibilities.

Phyllis Lovelock

O Lord, show me how to decide, and give me such trust in thee that I may receive thy guidance, and in calmness may act upon it.

Malcolm L. Playfoot

Sometimes, O God, when I think about growing up and leaving school I am excited and happy. At other times I begin to feel insecure, knowing I shall be out on my own, meeting new people and having to make my own way in the world. Please God, be my guide and helper, so that I make right decisions and face whatever comes with courage, cheerfulness and wisdom.

N.M.

Help me, O God, to spend wisely and to buy fairly, remembering that money and the things of this world are a trust for which I shall have to give an account to thee.

Malcolm L. Playfoot

Help us to earn money honestly
To spend a little wisely
To save some prudently
And to give generously.

Dear Father, I wish I could see you, then I would find it easier to believe in you. Where are you, God? I know I'm only one out of a great many people but I need your help. I've done so many things that are wrong, and have failed to do many things I ought to have done. Please forgive me, Father, and help me to do better.

N.M.

Lord, I cry for help in my wilderness,
The pressures, the temptations and the evils of daily life
   crowd in on me.

Give me the strength of will, Lord,
     to stand up for my faith
     when my school-friends talk of taking drugs
     and sleeping around, of drinking too much
     and not bothering about their work.
Save me from slipping into the mire of apathy,
     despondency, the uncaring, unhappy life
     of the unbeliever.

Lord, I find it so very hard to witness.
I am laughed and jeered at, like you were;

Called superstitious, childish, stupid . . .
Give me the strength, Lord, the reassurance
    of your presence,
      to try to set an example,
      to try to live a reasoned, contented life,
      to try to explain to uncaring people that
      this is not the only existence.

Dear Lord, please save me from becoming too smug,
    too complacent,
      deluded into thinking that I'm shielded from
      the rigours of life by the protection of a faith in you.
After all, you're no insurance policy against trouble, Lord.
Somehow I must learn to accept that,
Yet have faith that you will help me in trouble.

To have a living faith is no easy thing.
I know it's hard, Lord,
Hard to resist temptations,
Hard to say 'No' at the crucial moment,
Hard to live the sort of life I'm not ashamed for you to see,
    Lord.

Give me guidance, Lord,
Show me the right path to follow you.
Bolster me up when my faith flags and
    I will endeavour to serve you to the best of my ability
    all my days.

John E. Pugh Smith

Sometimes I feel you really love us and care about what happens to us, dear God, and then, when I think of all the people without homes and the children who have parents who are divorced, or who quarrel, I begin to wonder whether you really do care. How can we know that you do? I must and do believe in you, God. If I didn't I'd have no one to whom I could really turn with my problems.

When I think deeply enough I know why these things happen. You've let us choose how we live and whether we want to live peaceably. If you hadn't we would be like puppets and life would be very dull.

So thank you, God, for letting us choose what we do and how we live, but please help us all to choose the best things for the sake of everybody.

N.M.

O God, how can you really care about everybody. It's difficult to believe that you really know all about me and my problems. Do you really love me and care about what happens to me? I know the Bible has lots of stories about the way you go on seeking and caring even for those who have stopped loving you. There are those stories Jesus told about the prodigal son and the lost sheep and the lost piece of silver. Do you really care all that much about each of us, individually?

Although I'm asking you this I think I really *know* that you do care, but I can't understand how. Yet I can't understand how a computer works, or how men have found the way to the moon. So when I began to doubt I tell myself if men can make and do such clever things, how much greater and more wonderful you must be. So please. God, accept my love and thanks for all your care of me.

N.M.

I used to be so sure of you, God, and now I can't find you. I can't feel you are there, even when I pray. I don't know why it is unless it's because I've let a lot of other things crowd my life.

Please God let this dark, unhappy time pass. I want to find you again—I want to feel you there when I pray. Forgive me, and help me to get things straight again.

N.M.

My heart is filled with hostilities this morning, Lord.

Things have gone wrong in so many areas of my life.

So many people, all at once, have disappointed me, dismayed me, hurt me, let me down.

Lord, help me not to compound this sense of shock and pain by blaming you too. Help me to remember that, prayers or no prayers, how people act is not your fault. You are simply our creator, our confessor, our help, and our only true hope. And we, your creations, are so faulty and out of step with what you would have us be and do.

Lord, erase these hostilities from me so that I may approach this day in peace. Lord, help me not to put my faith in people, but in you.

Marjorie Holmes

Aren't parents difficult sometimes?

You should have heard the row we had last night.

What was it this time?

Oh—they said I stayed out too late—

They were worried sick—the usual thing.

Have you ever longed for a little flat on your own?

Yes—you bet—but to be honest I think I'd be lonely sometimes.

Yes, I expect you're right. There is something special about belonging to a family.

I know; I realise we're very lucky really to have parents who bother about us.

And after all, if parents *are* difficult, I expect we are too.

Let us give thanks to God for our homes and families and pray that we may grow in appreciation of all that we have been given in love and material blessings over the years. May we be kept from treating our homes as lodging houses and from showing insufficient concern for our parents. As we thank God for our homes we pray for all the homeless throughout the world.

We remember the homeless in this country and the work of Shelter. We think of all the refugees—keep their distress in our minds—it is so easy for 'refugee' to become just a word to us. We make this prayer in the name of Jesus who lived in a family in Nazareth.

K. A. Clegg

Lord, I want to be a living contact for you,
    a link between you and other people.
I've known you for so many years now,
    that I can recommend you to others who need you.

People do need you, Master, but they don't realise it.
They want to be happy and loved,
    to find a meaning to life.

They don't understand that only when lived with you
    can life find the truest expression.

They carry a hidden burden of conscience-distress
    and fail to see that only you can forgive sin
    and lift the load from them.

They complain of boredom and frustration, not knowing
    that you can add an extra dimension to their lives.

They are dissatisfied and unhappy, not realising that you
    can provide the missing ingredient.

So that is why, Lord, I want to be a living contact for you,
I want to tell people what you have done for me and others.

Sometimes I feel that I'd like to stand in the market-places
    of the world
    and shout aloud for all to hear;
    crying not my own wares, but yours.

Help me, Master, in my own way and just where I am,
    to be a living contact for you,
    a link between you and other people,
For they do need you.

Flora Larsson

Please give me courage, Lord. I'm frightened of so many things that people would call me a coward if they knew. I've never dared let anyone know how scared I am of being out alone in the dark. I'm afraid of burglars, afraid of storms and of getting hurt, or of anyone I love being injured or taken ill.

I wouldn't dare tell anyone but you about all this.

Please God, help me not to be so afraid and give me courage to face whatever comes.

N.M.

I saw it so clearly, Lord,
Through the words of one of your servants.
I have built hedges around my life
    without realising it.
    Higher and higher they have grown
    without my knowledge.

These hedges have shut others out and myself in.
It was comfortable so, comfortable and easy.

Less demanded of me,
Less expected of me,
Only myself to consider.

I have hedged about my time. *My* time!
Did I create time to be my own?
Have I sovereign right to twenty-four hours a day?
Is not each hour a token of your grace?

I have hedged about my leisure,
My free time is my own, I have said,
And I have miserly gloated over it,
Resenting any encroachment upon it.

I have hedged about my love,
These, and these only, I care for,
My nearest, my dearest, my friends,
All precious because they are *mine*.

Forgive me, Lord. Forgive my selfish living,
        my self-centredness
        my disregard of others.
    Help me to tear down the high hedges I have built,
And in their place to plan an open garden.
        Then I can look out
        and others can look in
    And we shall be drawn nearer to one another.
                                                Flora Larsson

Lord, another day of my life has gone and I know that
I have not used it as I could have done.
I have been selfish, tactless, thoughtless and unkind.
I have wanted too much for myself and forgotten my friends.
I have talked and talked, but I have not listened.
I have not listened to other people and now I do not know
    about their troubles and I cannot help them.

I have not listened, and therefore I cannot understand.
I have not stopped once all day, just to be quiet and listen to
  you either, Lord.

Lord, tomorrow you are going to give me another day.
Help me to use it better.
Tomorrow, Lord, help me to be quiet.

Virginia Salmon

THE PRAYER OF THE OX
> Dear God, give me time.
> Men are always so driven!
> Make them understand that I can never hurry,
>> Give me time to eat.
>> Give me time to plod.
>> Give me time to sleep.
>> Give me time to think.

Carmen Bernos de Gastold
Translated from the French by Rumer Godden

I went out, Lord,
Men were coming out.
They were coming and going,
Walking and running.
Everything was rushing, cars, lorries, the street, the whole
  town.
Men were rushing not to waste time.
They were rushing after time,
To catch up with time,
To gain time.

Goodbye sir, excuse me, I haven't time.
I'll come back, I can't wait, I haven't time.
I must end this letter—I haven't time.

I'd love to help you, but I haven't time.
I can't accept, having no time.
I can't think, I can't read, I'm swamped, I haven't time.
I'd like to pray, but I haven't time.

You understand, Lord, they simply haven't the time.
The child is playing, he hasn't time right now... Later on ...
The schoolboy has his homework to do, he hasn't time ...
    Later on ...
The student has his courses, and so much work, he hasn't
    time ...

    Later on ...
The young man is at his sports, he hasn't time... Later on ...
The young married man has his new house, he has to fix it up,
    he hasn't time ... Later on ...
The grandparents have their grandchildren, they haven't
    time ...
    Later on ...
They are ill, they have their treatments, they haven't time ...
    Later on ...
They are dying, they have no ...
Too late! ... They have no more time!

And so all men run after time, Lord.
They pass through life running—hurried, jostled, over-
    burdened, frantic, and they never get there. They haven't
    time.
In spite of all their efforts they're still short of time, of a great
    deal of time.
Lord, you must have made a mistake in your calculations.
There is a big mistake somewhere.
The hours are too short,
The days are too short,
Our lives are too short.

You who are beyond time, Lord, you smile to see us fighting it.
And you know what you are doing.
You make no mistakes in your distribution of time to men.
You give each one time to do what you want him to do.

But we must not lose time
    waste time,
    kill time,
For time is a gift that you give us,
But a perishable gift,
A gift that does not keep.

Lord, I have time,
I have plenty of time,
All the time that you give me.
The years of my life,
The days of my years,
The hours of my days,
They are all mine.
Mine to fill, quietly, calmly,
But to fill completely, up to the brim,
To offer them to you, that of their insipid water
You may make a rich wine such as you made once in Cana of
    Galilee.

I am not asking you tonight, Lord, for time to do this and
    then that,
But your grace to do conscientiously, in the time that you
    give me, what you want me to do.

Michel Quoist

There are some things I cannot talk about to anyone but you,
Lord—my secret longings—the things I'm not sure about—
my disappointments—my ambitions; but most of all, those
things I have done wrong, or which I've failed to do.

When I talk to you I need not to say these things aloud, but in the quietness and stillness of my mind, tell you about it. I can talk to you like this because I know you will understand, forgive, and help me to overcome.

Thank you, Lord.

N.M.

PRAYERS THROUGH
THE CENTURIES

Dear God,
Be good to me,
The sea is so wide
And my boat is so small.
A Prayer of the Breton Fishermen

O God, make us children of quietness and heirs of peace.
St. Clement First Century

All that we ought to have thought and have not thought,
All that we ought to have said and have not said,
All that we ought to have done and have not done;
All that we ought not to have thought and yet have thought,
All that we ought not to have spoken and yet have spoken,
All that we ought not to have done, and yet have done;
For these words, and works, pray we, O God,
     For forgiveness,
And repent with penance.
The Zendavesta. Ascribed to Zoroaster 1500 B.C.

Watch thou, dear Lord, with those who wake or watch or
weep tonight, and give thine angels charge over those who
sleep.

Tend thy sick ones, O Lord Christ, rest thy weary ones.
Bless thy dying ones. Soothe thy suffering ones.
Pity thine afflicted ones. Shield thy joyous ones. And all for
thy love's sake.

St. Augustine 354–430

O thou who art the light of the minds that know thee;
    the life of the souls that love thee:
    and the strength of the wills that serve thee;
Help us so to know thee that we may truly love thee;
    so to love thee that we may fully serve thee,
    whom to serve is perfect freedom;
    through Jesus Christ our Lord.
After St. Augustine 354–430 Gelasian Sacramentary

Lord, be with us this day.
Within us to purify us;
Above us to draw us up;
Beneath us to sustain us;
Before us to lead us;
Behind us to restrain us;
Around us to protect us.

St. Patrick 389–461

Christ be with me,
    Christ within me
Christ behind me
    Christ before me
Christ beside me
    Christ to win me
Christ to comfort and restore me
Christ beneath me
    Christ above me

Christ in quiet and
    Christ in danger
Christ in hearts of all that love me
Christ in mouth of friend and stranger.
St. Patrick 389–461

I bind unto myself today
The Power of God to hold and lead,
His eye to watch, his might to stay
His ear to harken to my need;
The wisdom of my God to teach,
His hand to guide, his shield to ward;
The word of God to give me speech,
His heavenly host to be my guard.
St. Patrick 389–461

May the strength of God pilot us.
May the power of God preserve us.
May the wisdom of God instruct us.
May the hand of God protect us.
May the way of God direct us.
May the shield of God defend us.
May the host of God guard us against the snares of evil and
    the temptations of the world.
St. Patrick's Breastplate 389–461

O Lord, our Saviour, who has warned us that thou wilt
require much of those to whom much is given; grant that we
whose lot is cast in so goodly a heritage may strive together
more abundantly by prayer and by every other means to
extend to others what we so richly enjoy, that as we have
entered into the labours of other men, we may so labour that

others in their turn may enter into ours, to the fulfilment of
thy holy will, and the salvation of all men.

Fourth Century

Bless all who worship thee,
From the rising of the sun
Unto the going down of the same.
Of thy goodness, give us;
With thy love, inspire us;
By thy spirit, guide us;
By thy power, protect us;
In thy mercy, receive us,
Now and always.

Fifth Century Collect

Into thy hands, O Lord, we commit ourselves this day.
Give to each one of us a watchful, a humble, and a diligent
spirit, that we may seek in all things to know thy will, and
when we know it may perform it perfectly and gladly, to the
honour and glory of thy name, through Jesus Christ our Lord.

Gelasian Sacramentary Fifth Century

O God, who art peace everlasting, whose chosen reward is
the gift of peace, and who hast taught us that the peace-
makers are thy children, pour thy peace into our souls, that
everything discordant may utterly vanish, and all that makes
for peace be loved and sought by us always.

Mozarabic Sacramentary Fifth Century

O gracious and holy Father,
give us wisdom to perceive thee,
intelligence to understand thee,
diligence to seek thee,

patience to wait for thee,
eyes to behold thee,
a heart to meditate upon thee,
and a life to proclaim thee;
through the power of the Spirit of Jesus Christ our Lord.

Attributed to St. Benedict 480–543

O Lord, give us, we beseech thee, in the name of Jesus Christ, that love which shall never cease, that will kindle our lamps but not extinguish them, that they may enlighten others and may we always desire thee.

St. Columba 521–597

Alone with none but thee, my God,
I journey on my way.
What need I fear, when thou art near
O king of night and day?
More safe am I within thy hand
Than if a host did round me stand.

St. Columba 521–597

O God, great and wonderful who has created the heavens, dwelling in the light and beauty thereof; who hast made the earth, revealing thyself in every flower that opens; let not mine eyes be blind to thee, neither let mine heart be dead, but teach me to praise thee, even as the lark which offereth her song at daybreak.

St. Isidore of Seville 560–636

Lord God Almighty, shaper and ruler of all creatures, we pray thee of thy great mercy to guide us to thy will, to make our minds steadfast, to strengthen us against temptation, to put far from us all unrighteousness. Shield us against our foes, seen and unseen, teach us that we may inwardly love thee before all things with a clean mind and a clean body. For thou art our maker and our redeemer, our help and our comfort, our trust and our hope, now and ever.

King Alfred 849–901

Grant, O our God, that we may know thee, love thee, and rejoice in thee; and if in this life we cannot do those things fully, grant that we may at the least progress in them from day to day, for Christ's sake.

St. Anselm 1033–1109

O Lord our God, grant us grace to desire thee with our whole heart, so that desiring thee we may seek and find thee; and so finding thee, may love thee; and loving thee, may hate those sins which separate us from thee, for the sake of Jesus Christ.

St. Anselm 1033–1109

O Lord, hear my prayer, fulfil my desire to my good and to the praise of thy holy name.

Sarum Breviary 1085

O Divine Master, grant that I may not so much seek
    to be consoled, as to console,
    to be understood, as to understand,
    to be loved, as to love;
    for it is in giving that we receive,
    it is in pardoning that we are pardoned,
    and it is in dying that we are born
    to eternal life.

St. Francis of Assisi 1182–1226

Lord make me an instrument of thy peace;
Where there is hatred, let me sow love;
Where there is injury, pardon;
Where there is discord, union;
Where there is doubt, faith;
Where there is despair, hope;
Where there is darkness, light;
Where there is sadness, joy.
                    St. Francis of Assisi 1182–1226

Thanks be to thee, our Lord Jesus Christ, for all the benefits which thou has given us; for all the pains and insults which thou hast borne for us.

O most merciful redeemer, friend and brother, may we know thee more clearly, love thee more dearly and follow thee more nearly, now and ever.
                    St. Richard of Chichester 1197–1233

Give me, O Lord, a steadfast heart,
    which no unworthy affection may drag downwards;
Give me an unconquered heart,
    which no tribulation can wear out;
Give me an upright heart,
    which no unworthy purpose may tempt aside.
Bestow upon me also, O Lord my God,
    understanding to know thee,
    diligence to seek thee,
    wisdom to find thee,
    and a faithfulness that may finally embrace thee.
                    St. Thomas Aquinas 1225–74

O God, Almighty Father, King of kings and Lord of lords, grant that the hearts and minds of all who go out as leaders before us, the statesmen, the judges, the men of learning and the men of wealth, may be so filled with the love of thy laws, and of that which is righteous and life-giving, that they may be worthy stewards of thy good and perfect gifts; through Jesus Christ our Lord.

Knights of the Garter Fourteenth Century

Grant us, O Lord, to know that which is worth knowing, to love that which is worth loving, to praise that which pleaseth thee most, to esteem that which is most precious unto thee, and to dislike whatsoever is evil in thine eyes. Grant us, with true judgment, to distinguish things that differ, and above all to search out and to do what is well pleasing unto thee, through Jesus Christ our Lord.

Thomas à Kempis 1380–1471

O Lord Jesus Christ, our maker and redeemer, who by thy providence hast made us what we are: thou hast a purpose for us; do thou, O Lord, in thy mercy, fulfil in us thy purpose. Thou alone art wisdom; thou knowest what may benefit sinners such as we are; do thou, in thy mercy, direct our future, according to thy will, as seemeth best in the eyes of thy majesty, O Jesus Christ, our Lord.

King Henry VI 1421–1471

O Lord Jesus Christ, who art the way, the truth and the life, we pray thee suffer us not to stray from thee, who art the way, nor to distrust thee, who art the truth, nor to rest on any other than thee, who art the life. Teach us what to believe, what to do and wherein to take our rest.

Erasmus 1467–1536

The things, good Lord, that we pray for, give us grace to work for; through Jesus Christ our Lord.

Sir Thomas More 1478–1535

Teach us, good Lord, to serve thee as thou deservest;
To give and not to count the cost;
To fight and not to heed the wounds;
To toil and not to seek for rest;
To labour and not to ask for any reward
Save that of knowing that we do thy will.

St. Ignatius Loyola 1491–1556

O most dear and tender Father, our defender and nourisher, endue us with thy grace, that we may cast off the great blindness of our minds, and carefulness of worldly things, and may put our whole study and care in keeping of thy holy law; and that we may labour and travail for our necessities in this life, like the birds of the air and the lilies of the field, without care. For thou hast promised to be careful for us; and hast commanded that upon thee we should cast our care, who livest and reignest, world without end.

King Henry VIII 1491–1547

God be in my head,
And in my understanding:
God be in mine eyes,
And in my looking:
God be in my mouth
And in my speaking;
God be in my heart,
And in my thinking;
God be at my end,
And at my departing.

Sixteenth Century Sarum Primer (1527)

O gracious God, and most merciful Father, which hast vouchsafed us the rich and precious jewel of thy holy word, assist us with thy Spirit, that it may be written in our hearts to our everlasting comfort, to reform us, to renew us according to thine own image, to build us up and edify us into the perfect building of thy Christ, sanctifying, and increasing in us all heavenly virtues. Grant this, O heavenly Father, for Jesus Christ's sake.

King Edward VI 1537–1553

O Lord God, when thou givest to thy servants to endeavour any great matter, grant us also to know that it is not the beginning but the continuing of the same until it be thoroughly finished which yieldeth the true glory.

Sir Francis Drake 1540–1596

Let this day, O Lord, add some knowledge or good deed to yesterday.

Lancelot Andrewes 1555–1626

Open thou mine eyes that I may see,
Incline my heart that I may desire,
Order my steps that I may follow
The way of thy commandments.
Lancelot Andrewes 1555–1626

O Lord, never suffer us to think that we can stand by ourselves, and not need thee.

John Donne 1573–1631

Into thy hands, O Lord, we commend our souls and bodies, beseeching thee to keep us this night under thy protection,

and to strengthen us for thy service on the morrow, for Christ's sake.

Archbishop Laud (adapted) 1573

O Lord, the Scripture says: 'There is a time for silence and a time for speech.' Saviour, teach me the silence of humility, the silence of wisdom, the silence of love, the silence of perfection, the silence that speaks without words, the silence of faith.

Lord, teach me to silence my own heart that I may listen to the gentle movement of the Holy Spirit within me and sense the depths which are of God.

Frankfurt Prayer—Sixteenth Century
Translated by B.G.

O merciful God, be thou now unto me a strong tower of defence, I humbly entreat thee. Give me grace to await thy leisure, and patiently to bear what thou doest unto me; nothing doubting or mistrusting thy goodness towards me; for thou knowest what is good for me better than I do. Therefore, do with me in all things what thou wilt; only arm me, I beseech thee, with thine armour, that I may stand fast; above all things taking to me the shield of faith; praying always that I may refer myself wholly to thy will, abiding thy pleasure, and comforting myself in those troubles which it shall please thee to send me, seeing such troubles are profitable for me; and I am assuredly persuaded that all thou doest cannot but be well; and unto thee be all honour and glory.

Lady Jane Grey 1537–1554

The eyes of all things do look up and trust in thee, O Lord, thou givest them their meat in due season, thou dost open thy hand and fillest with thy blessing everything living. Good

Lord, bless us and all thy gifts which we receive of thy
bountiful liberality; through Jesus Christ our Lord.

Queen Elizabeth I 1533–1603

Here a little child I stand,
Heaving up my either hand;
Cold as paddocks though they be,
Here I lift them up to thee,
For a benison to fall
On our meat and on us all.

Robert Herrick 1591–1674

(Paddocks are toads, or frogs: a benison is a blessing.)

Thou who hast given so much to me
Give one thing more, a grateful heart, for Christ's sake.

George Herbert 1593–1632

Teach us, our God and king,
In all things thee to see,
That what we do in anything
We do it unto thee.

George Herbert 1593–1632

Forgive me, Lord, for thy dear Son,
The ill that I this day have done,
That with the world, myself and thee,
I, ere I sleep, at peace may be.

Thomas Ken, Bishop 1637–1711

O Lord, thou knowest how busy I must be this day.
If I forget thee, do not thou forget me.

Sir Jacob Astley (before the battle of Edgehill, 1642)

Lord, help me to know that:
He who is down need fear no fall,
He that is low, no pride;
He that is humble ever shall
Have God to be his guide.

Make me content with what I have,
Little be it or much;
And, Lord, contentment ever crave,
Because thou savest such.
Adapted from John Bunyan 1628–88

O God, help us not to despise or oppose what we do not understand.
William Penn 1644–1718

O heavenly Father, subdue in me whatever is contrary to thy holy will. Grant that I may ever study to know thy will, that I may know how to please thee.

Grant, O God, that I may never run into those temptations which, in my prayers, I desire to avoid.

Lord never permit my trials to be above my strength.
Thomas Wilson 1663–1755

Almighty and Eternal God, the disposer of all the affairs in the world, there is not one circumstance so great as not to be subject to thy power, nor so small but it comes within thy care; thy goodness and wisdom show themselves through all thy works, and thy loving kindness and mercy appear in the several dispensations of thy providence. May we readily submit ourselves to thy pleasure and sincerely resign our wills to thine, with all patience, meekness, and humility, through Jesus Christ our Lord.
Queen Anne 1665–1714

Bless me, O Lord, and let my food strengthen me to serve thee, for Jesus Christ's sake.

Isaac Watts 1674–1748

O Lord, let us not live to be useless, for Christ's sake.

John Wesley 1703–1791

Jesus, strengthen my desire to work and speak and think for thee.

Charles Wesley 1707–1788

What thou shalt today provide,
Let me as a child receive;
What tomorrow may betide,
Calmly to thy wisdom leave.
'Tis enough that thou wilt care;
Why should I the burden bear?

John Newton 1725–1807

Grant us grace, Almighty Father, so to pray as to deserve to be heard.

Jane Austen 1775–1817

Make us to remember, O God, that every day is thy gift, and ought to be used according to thy command; through Jesus Christ our Lord.

Samuel Johnson 1709–1784

Let thy blessing, O Lord, rest upon our work this day. Teach us to seek after truth, and enable us to attain it; but grant that as we increase in the knowledge of earthly things, we may grow in the knowledge of thee, whom to know is life eternal; through Jesus Christ our Lord.

Adapted from Thomas Arnold 1795–1842

Most loving Lord, give me a childlike love of thee, which may cast out all fear.

Canon E. B. Pusey 1800–82

Teach us, O Father, how to ask thee each moment silently for thy help. If we fail, teach us at once to ask thee to forgive us. If we are disquieted, enable us, by thy grace, quickly to turn to thee. May we will, do and say just what thou, our loving and tender Father, willest us to will, do and say. Work thy holy will in us, and through us, this day. Protect us, guide us, bless us within and without, that we may do something this day for love of thee; something which shall please thee; and that we may this evening be nearer to thee, though we see it not nor know it. Lead us, O Lord, in a straight way unto thyself, and keep us in thy grace unto the end, through Jesus Christ our Lord.

Canon E. B. Pusey 1800–1882

For flowers that bloom about our feet,
Father, we thank thee.
For tender grass so fresh, so sweet,
Father, we thank thee.
For the song of bird and hum of bee,
For all things fair we hear or see,
Father in heaven, we thank thee.

For blue of stream and blue of sky
Father we thank thee.
For pleasant shade of branches high
Father, we thank thee.

For fragrant air and cooling breeze,
For the beauty of the blooming trees,
Father in heaven, we thank thee.

For this new morning with its light,
Father, we thank thee.
For rest and shelter of the night,
Father we thank thee.
For health and food, for love and friends,
For everything thy goodness sends,
Father in heaven, we thank thee.
Ralph Waldo Emerson 1803–1882

Drop thy still dews of quietness,
Till all our strivings cease:
Take from our souls the strain and stress,
And let our ordered lives confess
The beauty of thy peace.
John Greenleaf Whittier 1807–1892

O Lord, give us more charity (love), more self-denial, more likeness to thee. Teach us to sacrifice our comforts to others, and our likings for the sake of doing good. Make us kindly in thought, gentle in word, generous in deed. Teach us that it is better to give than to receive, better to forget ourselves than to put ourselves forward; better to minister than to be ministered unto.
Henry Alford 1810–1871

O God, who hast made of one blood all nations of men for to dwell on the face of the earth, and didst send thy blessed Son, Jesus Christ, to preach peace to them that are afar off, and to them that are nigh; grant that all the peoples of the world may feel after thee and find thee; and hasten, O God, the fulfilment of thy promise, to pour out thy Spirit upon all flesh; through Jesus Christ our Lord.

Bishop Cotton of Calcutta 1813–1866

Guide us, teach us, and strengthen us, O Lord, we beseech thee, until we become such as thou wouldst have us be; pure, gentle, truthful, high-minded, courteous, generous, able, dutiful and useful; for thy honour and glory.

Charles Kingsley 1819–1875

Take from us, O heavenly Father, all pride and vanity, all boasting and forwardness, and give us the true courage that shows itself by gentleness; the true wisdom that shows itself by simplicity; and the true power that shows itself by modesty and thought for others; through Jesus Christ our Lord.

Charles Kingsley 1819–1875

We let the world overcome us; we live too much in continual fear of the chances and changes of mortal life. We let things go too much their own way. We try too much to get what we can by our own selfish wits, without considering our neighbour. We follow too much the ways and fashions of the day, doing and saying and thinking anything that comes uppermost, just because there is so much around us. Free us from our selfish interests, and guide us, good Lord, to see your way, and to do your will.

Charles Kingsley 1819–1875

O God, in whom we live and move and have our being, open our eyes that we may behold thy fatherly presence ever about us. Teach us to be anxious for nothing, and when we have done what thou hast given us to do, help us, O God, our

Saviour, to leave the issue to thy wisdom, knowing that all things are possible to us through thy son our Saviour, Jesus Christ.

R. M. Benson 1825–1915

Almighty God and most merciful Father, who hast given us a new commandment that we should love one another, give us also grace that we may fulfil it. Make us gentle, courteous and forbearing. Direct our lives so that we may look each to the good of the other in word and deed. And hallow all our friendships by the blessing of thy Spirit, for his sake who loved us, and gave himself for us, Jesus Christ our Lord.

Bishop Westcott 1825–1901

Make us of quick and tender conscience, O Lord, that understanding, we may obey every word of thine this day, and discerning, may follow every suggestion of thine indwelling Spirit.

Christina Rossetti 1830–1894

O Lord, whose way is perfect, help us, we pray thee, always to trust in thy goodness, that walking with thee and following thee in all simplicity, we may possess quiet and contented minds, and may cast all our care on thee, who carest for us. Grant this, O Lord, for thy dear Son's sake, Jesus Christ.

Christina Rossetti 1830–1894

Speak, Lord, for thy servant heareth.
Grant us ears to hear
Eyes to see,

Wills to obey,
Hearts to love;
Then declare what thou wilt,
Reveal what thou wilt,
Command what thou wilt,
Demand what thou wilt.
Christina Rossetti 1830–1894

O Lord God, grant us always, whatever the world may say, to content ourselves with what thou wilt say, and to care only for thine approval, which will outweigh all words; for Jesus Christ's sake.
General Gordon 1833–1885

Make us ever eager, Lord, to share the good things that we have. Grant us such a measure of thy Spirit that we may find more joy in giving than in getting. Make us ready to give cheerfully without grudging, secretly without praise, and in sincerity without looking for gratitude, for Jesus Christ's sake.
John Hunter 1849–1917

The day returns and brings us the petty round of irritating concerns and duties. Help us to play the man, help us to perform them with laughter and kind faces, let cheerfulness abound with industry. Give us to go blithely on our business all this day, bring us to our resting beds weary and content and undishonoured, and grant us in the end the gift of sleep.
Robert Louis Stevenson 1850–1894

When the day returns call us up with morning faces, and with morning hearts, eager to labour, happy if happiness be our portion, and if the day is marked for sorrow, strong to endure.

> *Robert Louis Stevenson 1850–1894*
> (Written and read to his family by R.L.S.
> on the eve of his non-anticipated death)

Give me courage, and gaiety, and the quiet mind.
> *Robert Louis Stevenson 1850–1894*

Almighty God, from whom all thoughts of truth and peace proceed, kindle, we pray thee, in the hearts of all men, the true love of peace, and guide with thy pure and peaceable wisdom those who take counsel for the nations of the earth; that in tranquility thy kingdom may go forward, till the earth be filled with the knowledge of thy love; through Jesus Christ our Lord.

> *Francis Paget 1851–1911*

> Through every minute of this day,
>   Be with me, Lord!
> Through every day of all this week,
>   Be with me, Lord!
> Through every week of all this year,
>   Be with me, Lord!
> Through all the years of all this life,
>   Be with me, Lord!
> So shall the days and weeks and years
> Be threaded on a golden cord,
> And all draw on with sweet accord
> Unto thy fulness, Lord
> That so, when time is past,
> By grace, I may at last,
>   Be with thee, Lord.
> *John Oxenham 1853–1941*

Lord, give me faith!—to live from day to day,
With tranquil heart to do my simple part,
And, with my hand in thine, just go thy way.

Lord, give me faith!—to trust, if not to know,
With quiet mind in all things thee to find,
And, child-like, go where thou wouldst have me go.

Lord, give me faith!—to leave it all to thee,
The future is thy gift, I would not lift
The veil thy love has hung 'twixt it and me.

John Oxenham 1853–1941

O God, within whose sight
All men have equal right
To worship thee,
Break every bar that holds
Thy flock in diverse folds;
Thy will from none withholds
Full liberty.

Lord, set thy churches free
From foolish rivalry;
Lord, set us free!
Let all past bitterness
Now and for ever cease,
And all our souls possess
Thy charity!

Lord, set the people free!
Let all men draw to thee
In unity!
Thy temple courts are wide,
Therein, let all abide
In peace, and side by side
Serve only thee!

God, grant us now thy peace!
Bid all dissensions cease!
God, send us peace!
Peace in true liberty,
Peace in Equality,
Peace and Fraternity,
God, send us peace!

John Oxenham 1853–1941

God of the busy daytime;
God of the quiet night;
Whose peace pervades the darkness
And greets us with the light.
Save with thy presence near us
Wherever we may be,
Thou, God, our great protector
We love and worship thee.

John Oxenham 1853–1941

Gracious God, remember us, we beseech thee, in our work
this day. If it be thy will, give unto us a prosperous day.
May all our work be well done. May we turn nothing out half
done. May we glorify thee by honest good work; for the sake
of him who completed his work for us, even Jesus Christ our
Lord.

Rev. J. H. Jowett 1864–1923

Grant us the will to fashion as we feel,
Grant us the strength to labour as we know,
Grant us the purpose, ribb'd and edged with steel,
To strike the blow.

Knowledge we ask not—knowledge thou hast lent,
But Lord, the will—there lies our bitter need,
Give us to build above the deep intent.
    The deed, the deed.

John Drinkwater 1882–1937

O Christ who holds the open gate,
O Christ who drives the furrow straight,
O Christ, the plough, O Christ, the laughter,
Of holy white birds flying after,   .
Lo, all my heart's field red and torn,
And thou wilt bring the young green corn
The young green corn divinely springing,
The young green corn for ever singing;
And when the field is fresh and fair
Thy blessed feet shall glitter there,
And we will walk the weeded field
And tell the golden harvest's yield,
The corn that makes the holy bread
By which the soul of man is fed,
The holy bread, the food unpriced,
The everlasting mercy, Christ.

John Masefield 1878–1967

Here, Lord, is my life. I place it on the altar today. Use it as you will.

Albert Schweitzer 1875–1965

Grant me, O Lord, the royalty of inward happiness and the serenity which comes from living close to thee. Daily renew in me the sense of joy, and let the eternal Spirit of the Father dwell in my soul and body so that, bearing about with me the infection of a good courage, I may be a diffuser of life, and may meet all ills and cross accidents with gallant and high-hearted happiness, giving thee thanks always for all things.

L. H. M. Soulsby Twentieth Century 1856–1927

God grant me the serenity
To accept the things I cannot change,
The courage to change the things I can,
And the wisdom to know the difference.
Rev. Dr. Reinhold Niebuhr 1892–1971

O God, who hast bound us together in this bundle of life, give us grace to understand how our lives depend on the courage, the industry, the honesty and integrity of our fellow men; that we may be mindful of their needs, grateful for their faithfulness, and faithful in our responsibilities to them; through Jesus Christ our Lord.

Rev. Dr. Reinhold Niebuhr 1892–1971

GRACES

Thank you for the world so sweet
Thank you for the food we eat,
Thank you for the birds that sing,
Thank you, God, for everything.
Mrs. E. Rutter Leatham

For these and for all thy gifts, we give thee thanks, O God.

God bless our meat,
God guide our ways,
God give us grace our Lord to please.
Lord long preserve in peace and health
Our gracious Queen Elizabeth.

(1565)

Some ha'e meat, and canna eat,
    And some wad eat that want it;
But we ha'e meat, and we can eat,
    And sae the Lord be thankit.
Robert Burns

Bless these thy gifts, most gracious God
From whom all goodness springs,

Make clean our hearts and feed our souls
　　With good and joyful things.

　Lord, bless this food for our use and us in thy service, and
help us to remember the needs of others; for Christ's sake.

SUBJECT INDEX

167

ACKNOWLEDGMENTS

The compiler and the publishers are grateful to the following for permission to include prayers in this anthology:

Allans of Melbourne, for a prayer by Brother William.

Mrs. L. A. Anson, for the prayer from *New Every Morning*, by Canon Anson, published by the British Broadcasting Corporation.

The Rev. Dr. Leonard P. Barnett, for a prayer from *A Prayer Diary for Youth*, published by the Methodist Church Division of Education and Youth.

A. & C. Black, Ltd., for a prayer by Albert Schweitzer.

Blackie & Son, for prayers from *A Morning Assembly Book*, compiled by J. W. and S. Brimer.

Blandford Press, for prayers from *Infant Teachers' Prayer Book* and *Junior Teachers' Prayer Book*, compiled by D. M. Prescott, and for the prayers by E. Gould, E.R., and B.B.

Curtis Brown Ltd., for the quotation from *Morning Prayer* from *The New Nutcracker Suite and Other Innocent Verses*. © 1962 by Ogden Nash.

Beryl Bye, for prayers from *Please God*, published by Church Pastoral Aid Society (CPAS).

Geoffrey Chapman for the prayer from *Everyday Prayer Book*.

Christian Education Movement (CEM), by permission of Rev. John Sutcliffe, General Secretary, for three prayers.

Church Information Office, for a prayer from *God Is Looking After Me*, published in aid of handicapped children; for prayers from *In Excelsis*, compiled by H. W. Dobson, including prayers by H. Widdows and Mrs. Lesbia Scott; for prayers from *Live and Pray* and *Pray With*, compiled by Brother Kenneth and Sister Geraldine; and for a prayer from *Prayer-time with Juniors*.

Church Missionary Society, for prayers from *All Our Days*, by Irene Taylor and Phyllis Garlick.

Church Pastoral Aid Society, for prayers from *Prayers for Today's Church*, compiled by Dick Williams. Permission given by the following, whose prayers are included:

ACKNOWLEDGMENTS

Gordon Bates, M. H. Botting from his collection, Ian Bunting, K. A. Clegg, Timothy Dudley-Smith, Christopher Idle, Patricia Mitchell, J. D. Searle, Dick Williams; also a prayer from *God Thoughts*, by Dick Williams.

Dr. Donald Coggan, the Archbishop of Canterbury, for the prayer on page 80.

William Collins Sons & Co., Ltd., and Elfrida Vipont, for a prayer from *Bless This Day* and one by Bishop E. S. Woods.

Peter Davies, for prayers from *The Prayers of Peter Marshall*, by Catherine Marshall.

Dragon School, for a prayer from *Hymns and Prayers for Dragons*.

Miss Theo Dunkerley, for prayers from *Bees in Amber*, by John Oxenham, published by Methuen & Co., Ltd.; from *First Prayers for Children*, by John Oxenham and Roderic Dunkerley; and for the extract from the novel *The Man Who Would Save the World*, by John Oxenham, published by Longmans.

Evans Brothers Ltd., for prayers from *Child Education*, by A. W. L. Chitty and Mary Osborn.

The Trustees of The Fellowship Hymn Book, for a prayer by S. W. Meyer, from *The Fellowship Hymn Book*.

Fontana Paperbacks, for prayers from *Prayers for the Family*, by Rita Snowden; and for prayers from *The Plain Man's Book of Prayers*, by William Barclay.

Gill and Macmillan Ltd., for a prayer from *Prayers of Life*, by Michel Quoist.

Hodder & Stoughton, for prayers from *Prayers for Children*, by Brenda Holloway; for prayers from *Just a Moment, Lord*, by Flora Larsson; for prayers from *Uncommon Prayers* and *Uncommon Prayers for Young People*, compiled by Cecil Hunt, including prayers by Thomas Henry Basil Webb, Richard Molesworth Dennis, F. W. Faber, T.T., and Margaret Bailey; and for prayers from *I've Got to Talk to Somebody, Lord*, by Marjorie Holmes.

Holt, Rinehart & Winston, Inc., for a prayer from *Are You Running with Me, Jesus?* by Malcolm Boyd. Copyright © 1965 by Malcolm Boyd.

Michael Joseph, for an extract from *Silver Sand and Snow*, by Eleanor Farjeon.

Lutterworth Press, for a prayer from *Stories of Jesus for Mothers to Tell*, by Elfreyda M. C. Wightman; and for prayers from *A Book of Prayers for Boys and Girls*, by the same author; for prayers from *Family Prayers*, by A. Murray Smith; and for prayers from *Children Pray*, by Ella Forsyth Wright.

Macmillan Publishing Co., Inc., for lines from "The Everlasting Mercy," in *Poems*, by John Masefield. Copyright 1912 by Macmillan Publishing Co., Inc.; renewed 1940 by John Masefield.

Mayhew McCrimmon, Great Wakering, Essex, for prayers from *It's Me, O*

Lord, by Michael Hollings and Etta Gullick, and for prayers from *The One Who Listens*, by the same authors; also a prayer by A. G. Bullivant.

The Methodist Church Division of Education and Youth, for prayers from *Orders of Service for Family Worship*, compiled by Doris W. Street; for prayers from *Hear My Prayer*, by J. M. Macdougall Ferguson; for a prayer from the *Junior Service Book*, by Doris W. Street; and for prayers from *Youth at Worship*, by Godfrey S. Pain.

Methodist Publishing House, for prayers by Walter Rauschenbusch and R. J. Shambrook, from *A Book of Worship for Schools*, compiled by H. F. Matthews.

Moorhouse-Barlow Co., Inc., for prayers from *So Help Me God*, by Geddes MacGregor.

A. R. Mowbray & Co., Ltd., for prayers from *Talking to God*, by Ena V. Martin; and for a prayer by Father Andrew, from *Prayers from Father Andrew*.

John Murray (Publishers) Ltd., for prayers from *A Chain of Prayer*, compiled by Selina Fitzherbert Fox and including a prayer by Selina Fitzherbert Fox.

The National Christian Education Council, for a prayer from *Prayers for Home and Family*, by Leslie R. Earnshaw; for prayers from *Praying with Beginners*, by Christopher and Margaret Bacon, and for prayers from *Praying with Juniors*, by Jack and Edna Young.

Nottingham General Hospital and the Senior Nursing Officer, for prayers from *Prayers for Use in Hospitals*.

Oxford University Press, for prayers from *A Book of Prayers for Schools*, including prayers by Evelyn Underhill, William de Witt Hyde, A. G. Pite, a prayer from *The Kingdom, the Power and the Glory*, and a prayer for use at the London Hospital; for prayers from *Little Prayers*, by Virginia Kimber, *Prayers and Hymns for Junior Schools*, by G. W. Briggs and A. M. Ammon; for prayers from *The Daily Service*, compiled by G. W. Briggs, including prayers by G. W. Briggs, Rebecca Weston, and S. W. Meyer.

Saint Andrew Press, for prayers from *Sunday, Monday*, by R. S. Macnicol.

The Scripture Union, for prayers from *Let's Talk to God*, by Zinnia Bryan.

Sidgwick & Jackson Ltd., for an extract from *The Collected Poems of John Drinkwater*, Volume I.

Skeffington, for a prayer from *A Book of Prayers for Boys*, compiled by Rev. E. L. Bevan.

Society for the Promotion of Christian Knowledge (S.P.C.K.), for a prayer from *A Little Book of Praises*, by Lilian Cox; for a prayer from *Growing Up*, by Vivyen Bremner; prayers from *A St. Francis Prayer Book*, by Malcolm Playfoot;

ACKNOWLEDGMENTS

prayers from *A Brownie Guide Prayer Book*, by Rosalie Wakefield, including a prayer by Vivyen Bremner.

Student Christian Movement Press, for a prayer by B.D.M. from *A Book of Prayers for Young People*; for prayers from *A Book of Prayers for Schools*, including prayers by John Hunter, M. L. Jacks, H. Bisseker, Hugh Martin, E. M. Venables, and a prayer from *Abbotsholme (1935) Prayer Book* and one from *Hymns and Prayers for Dragons*, by permission of The Headmaster; and a prayer from *A Prayer Book for Boys and Girls*, by Margaret Cropper.

Toc H, for the *Toc H Prayer*, by George Moore; for prayers by the Rev. Bob Knight and John Hunter from *Yours in the Glory*, by Rev. Bob Knight of Toc H.

The United Society for the Propagation of the Gospel (U.S.P.G.), for prayers from *Young Christians at Prayer* and a prayer from *Prayer Is My Life*, by Margaret Dewey.

The Viking Press, Inc., for *Prayers from the Ark*, by Carmen Bernos de Gasztold, translated by Rumer Godden. Copyright © 1962 by Rumer Godden.

Henry Z. Walck Inc., for a prayer from *First Prayers*, by Tasha Tudor.

H. E. Walter, for prayers from *Little Prayers for Little People*, by Kathleen Partridge.

Wheaton, for prayers from *Gateways to Worship*, by Lilian Cox.

The text of the 1662 Book of Common Prayer is Crown Copyright and the extracts used herein are reproduced by permission.

Acknowledgment is also made to the following authors of prayers previously unpublished:

Sally Cawley, Mary Drewery, Hope Freeman, Nina Hinchy, Phyllis Lovelock, Graham Salmon, Virginia Salmon, John E. Pugh Smith, Jean Stevens, and Jane Vansittart. Also to Lilian Cox for a number of her unpublished prayers.

To all these, and to those who have so kindly lent me their own collection of prayers, I express my indebtedness. In particular I wish to express my appreciation of the valuable help of Phyllis Lovelock in assisting the checking of the sources and preparing indices. Some of her prayers are included in this collection.

Every effort has been made to trace the owners of copyright material. If, unwittingly, any copyright has been infringed, the compiler offers her apology.

INDEX OF SOURCES

INDEX OF FIRST PHRASES